EURIPIDES

The Trojan Women · Helen · The Bacchae

Revenge III

TRANSLATIONS FROM GREEK AND ROMAN AUTHORS

TRANSLATIONS FROM GREEK AND ROMAN AUTHORS

Series Editor: GRAHAM TINGAY

EURIPIDES

The Trojan Women · Helen · The Bacchae

Translated by NEIL CURRY

CAMBRIDGE UNIVERSITY PRESS

Cambridge
London   New York   New Rochelle
Melbourne   Sydney

Published by the Press Syndicate of the University of Cambridge
The Pitt Building, Trumpington Street, Cambridge CB2 1RP
32 East 57th Street, New York, NY 10022, USA
296 Beaconsfield Parade, Middle Park, Melbourne 3206, Australia

First published 1981

Photoset and printed in Great Britain by
REDWOOD BURN LIMITED, Trowbridge, Wiltshire, and
bound by Pegasus Bookbinding, Melksham, Wiltshire.

ISBN 0 521 28047 8

Permission to perform Neil Curry's translations of Euripides' *Trojan
Women*, *Helen* and *The Bacchae* should be obtained from Jan Van Loewen
Ltd., 21 Kingly Street, London W1R 5LB and suite 1400, 1501
Broadway, New York, NY 10036, USA.

British Library Cataloguing in Publication Data
Euripides
Helen, The Trojan Women, The Bacchae.
– (Translations from Greek and Roman
authors)
I. Title   II. Euripides. Trojan Women
III. Euripides. Bacchae   IV. Series
882'.01   PA3975.A2
ISBN 0 521 28047 8

The cover picture shows the head of the god, Dionysus, from an
illustration on a Greek storage jar. It is reproduced by courtesy of the
Hirmer Fotoarchiv.

For Natasha and Victoria

Contents

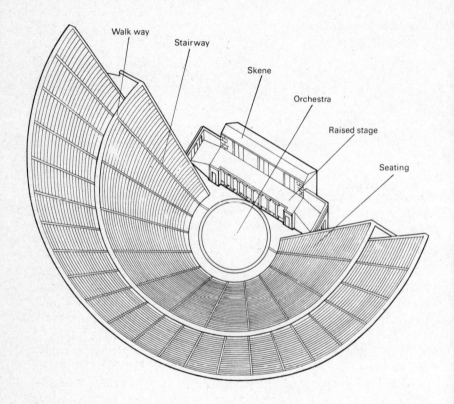

Plan of a Greek theatre

GREEK THEATRE

The setting of the great majority of Greek plays is in the open air, in front of a palace or a temple, because the Greeks spent most of their days out of doors, and the plays they watched were performed in open-air theatres. The most famous, the Theatre of Dionysus, was set into the hillside of the Acropolis at Athens and had a vast semi-circular auditorium, capable of seating about 14,000 people on tiers of wooden benches which rose from a level acting-area: this was a circle some sixty feet in diameter (called the *orchestra* or 'dancing place'). Behind this was a *skene*, or stage-house, from which the actors would enter, and on top of which the gods could appear. The actors spoke their lines in front of the *skene*, which represented the temple, or whatever building the play required; apart from this there was none of the scenery which we find in theatres today. Instead, there was that special kind of emptiness which allows the imagination to be carried away by the sounds of the words, for these, remember, were plays intended to be performed, not simply read. This direct appeal to the audience's imagination rather than to their eyes explains why the most dramatic events in Greek plays do not happen on the stage but are reported, often by a messenger. The sea-fight in *Helen*, or the horrific killing in *The Bacchae*, could not be enacted on any stage, but to the mind's eye they are actual, vivid and alive, thanks to Euripides' words.

The structure of the plays, with these long messengers' speeches, and their distinctly separate episodes, divided by choruses, may seem to us to be very formal, even to the extent of being ritualistic. This is because they did in fact develop out of the rituals of religion, and in particular out of the hymns sung at the festivals held to honour Dionysus, the great god of wine and fertility. These hymns, it is believed, developed into choral dances which acted out episodes from the Dionysus legend, and to them was later added a speaking part, where one actor told the story, using masks to represent the different characters. In the fifth century BC, Aeschylus, the earliest of the ancient Greek playwrights whose work has sur-

1

vived, introduced a second actor, and so conflict, the basis of all
real drama, began. With the plays of Sophocles, a third actor then
appeared, allowing for a fuller exploration of more complex *human*
relationships, and as this happened so the primary religious
element began to fade; indeed conventional religious belief was
even challenged by Euripides, the third great Athenian dramatist,
who portrayed his characters with even greater realism.

Theatre, even in Euripides' times, never became entirely separated
from religion; plays were only performed during the religious festivals, especially the one known as the Great Dionysia, which was
held in Athens at the end of March. But it was not only a festival in
the religious sense; there was, as in our music and drama festivals
today, a competitive element in it too. Three dramatists would
compete on three separate days, each entering three tragedies and
a comedy, which was known as a Satyr Play, and, at the end, a
panel of judges from the audience voted to decide the winner.

The actors, who were always men, continued to wear masks
because there were never more than three of them and conse-
quently they often had to play more than one part. However, it is
now known that the image of Greek actors in thick-soled boots,
padded clothing and grossly exaggerated masks represents the
practice of a very much later age. In Euripides' time they would
have worn something much nearer to normal, everyday tunics and
robes, though perhaps more brilliantly coloured; and the members
of the Chorus would certainly have needed costumes which
allowed freedom of movement, because their singing and dancing
remained a fundamental part of the performance, although their
dramatic significance had dwindled somewhat. The Chorus is
probably still the most distinctive feature of Greek tragedy, and the
one which a modern audience finds it most difficult to accept. The
Chorus performed many different functions, of course, but it may
perhaps best be seen as an intermediary between the playwright
and his audience. It has been called 'the ideal spectator', its
moods, views and reactions being in general those that the playwright wishes to generate in his audience.

In the fifth century BC the Chorus numbered fifteen, often
divided into two groups with a leader who had a solo part, but in
productions today, when choral speaking is rather out of favour, it

is usual to sub-divide it even further with a far greater use of solo voices, and this is certainly the intention in these versions.

Euripides' life spanned the fifth century BC (c.485 – c.406). Socrates and Pericles were his contemporaries, and he shared their interest in scientific speculation and what we would now call sociology. He lived through most of the Great War fought between Athens and Sparta (431 – 404 BC), and *The Trojan Women* and *Helen* reflect his weariness with the war and the brutality that accompanied it. It is likely that his criticism of accepted views about religion and the war led to his departure from Athens in 408 BC to the court of King Archelaus of Macedon, where he wrote *The Bacchae*.

Note: the small numbers in heavy type which occur in the texts of the plays indicate a note of explanation to be found at the end of that play.

The Trojan Women

The Legend
The Trojan Women scarcely has a plot. The play simply dwells on
and enlarges one brief moment at the end of the Trojan War. It
was a war which had begun when Paris, one of the sons of Priam,
the King of Troy, was set the task of deciding which of three goddesses – Aphrodite, Hera, and Pallas Athene – was the most
beautiful. All three offered him bribes, but he accepted Aphrodite's. She had offered him the most beautiful woman in the world:
Helen, wife of Menelaus, King of Sparta. When Menelaus found
that his wife had been carried off to Troy by Paris, he raised an
army that besieged Troy for the next ten years, the siege finally
being broken by the cunning strategy of the wooden horse. After
that came a massacre, and when the play opens all the Trojan men
are dead, and the women and children are waiting to be shipped
into slavery.

In his endeavour to show us the brutality of war, Euripides con-
centrates attention on the fate of individuals. First we see Hecuba,
the widow of King Priam, and share her grief as she learns that the
sacred virginity of her daughter Cassandra is to be violated by
Agamemnon; that another daughter, Polyxena, has already been
sacrificed at the tomb of Achilles; and then that Astyanax, her
grandson, the child of Troy's greatest hero, Hector, is to be flung
from the city walls to prevent him becoming a figure-head for any
future Trojan resurgence. After this comes the dramatic meeting of
Menelaus and Helen. All the women hate Helen, and Hecuba
wants her put to death instantly, but Menelaus weakens and takes
her back to Greece with him. So Hecuba has lost everything. All
that is left now is for her to see to the burial of Astyanax and get
ready to leave as the Greeks finally set fire to her city.

The Play
The structure of the play is decidedly episodic, but then, unlike
Helen, or *The Bacchae*, it does not set out to tell a story. There is no
kind of dénouement, and this part of the legend is of no great significance. For its first audience, in 415 BC, the overriding import-

4

ance of *The Trojan Women* was its contemporary relevance. Athens had, at that time, been sporadically at war with Sparta, with varying success, for sixteen years. Many people were opposed to the war, and in 416 BC an event occurred that shocked them deeply. The tiny island of Melos, with a population of less than 1,000, was ordered to assist the Athenian war effort with money and men. Amazingly, the Melians refused, saying that they preferred to remain neutral. Athens' reply was an invasion force that slaughtered every man on the island and sold the women and children into slavery. *The Trojan Women* was performed only three months later and the parallel must have been all too clear. What is more, a major naval expedition against Sicily was also being prepared at the same time and the lines about divine retribution being directed against a great fleet would have seemed uncomfortably ominous. The play is not, however, only a veiled reference to something that happened a long time ago; it remains a powerfully dramatic exposé of the brutalities of war, and of pompous nobodies, like Menelaus, who are responsible for them. It therefore seemed hardly surprising in 1968, when a military junta seized power in Greece, that Euripides should have been banned on the grounds that his plays were 'subversive'. After almost two and a half millennia, he was still a political force.

The Trojan Women

CHARACTERS

Poseidon	the god of the sea
Athene	daughter of Zeus, a battle-goddess who had favoured Greece
Hecuba	Queen of Troy
Chorus	of captive Trojan women
Talthybius	Herald of the Greek army
Cassandra	daughter of Hecuba
Andromache	widow of Hecuba's son, Hector, the champion of Troy
Astyanax	her son
Menelaus	a general of the Greek army
Helen	his wife

The plain between Troy and the Greek ships, in the darkness before dawn. A huge figure becomes visible.

Poseidon   My name is Poseidon. I am the god
Of the seas, and of the ocean.[1]
From under the waters of the Aegean
I have come, from those depths
Where sea-nymphs dance,
Weaving subtle patterns through the weeds.
I have come to Troy; my city.
For Apollo and I, we made it,
Every stone in those walls, every tower,
Straight and true, we built them.
Troy and its people were my especial care.
And now it is in ruins. Smoke
And rubble only; crushed
By the armies of Greece, and
By Athene. For it was she

6

Who urged Epius the Phocian
To build that horse, to line its belly with steel;
A secret and a silent death
Within a wooden horse, that strode
Between the walls of Troy.   20
Men will not forget.

The sacred groves are deserted;
The shrines are wet with blood;
On the steps of the altar of the almighty god
Priam the king lies dead,
While in the harbours the Greeks
Are loading their ships with gold;
Plunder and loot now all the riches of Troy.
It is ten long, wasted years since they sailed from
    Greece
To sack this city, and now
They have only to wait for a following wind,
And they will see their wives again.
Hera and Athene have won,
And I, too, must go,
For there is no man left to worship me.
Sickness in a city strikes also at the gods,
And desolation is the end of religion.
There are women weeping on the banks of
    Scamander
Where the troops drew lots for them.
They are to be shipped away as slaves   40
To Thessaly, and Athens and Arcady.
While those who have yet to be assigned
To their new masters have been put into tents,
And must wait for the general
To decide what is to become of them.
There too, guarded like the rest, is Helen.

But, if any man would see misery itself,
Then it is here. Here, weeping as many tears
As she has griefs to bear, lies Hecuba.
Her husband and her sons are dead;
Her daughter, whom the Lord Apollo loved,
Yet spared and blessed with prophecy,

Cassandra, in defiance of the gods,
Is to be raped by Agamemnon.
Yet still this grief is not complete.
For there is no one dares to tell her
That even while she lay here weeping on the
    ground,
Polyxena, her youngest child,
Was most pitifully slain –
A human sacrifice at great Achilles' grave.   60

O then farewell, my city, farewell.
Your battlements, your shining towers,
But for the hatred of Pallas Athene,
They might still be standing now.

A second huge figure is seen standing near by.

Athene	Poseidon, my father's brother, a great god,
	And honoured among the gods, may one,
	Formerly at bitter enmity with you,
	Now be allowed to speak, and offer peace?
Poseidon	You may speak, most noble Athene,
	The claims of kinship cannot lightly be denied.
Athene	I thank you for your courtesy, my Lord.
	This is a matter to concern us both.
Poseidon	Some message from the gods? From Zeus
	perhaps?
Athene	No. I have come – to request your assistance:
	Your power, allied with mine – for the sake of
	Troy.
Poseidon	Athene, whose hatred brought ruin to Troy?
	Has the sight of its ashes moved her to pity?
Athene	My sometime deeds are not at issue here.
	Will the might of Poseidon aid my endeavour?
Poseidon	First, I must know exactly what it is 80
	That you 'endeavour', and whether it is truly
	For the sake of Troy – or subtly favours Greece.
Athene	Would not my former enemies in Troy rejoice
	If, on their voyage home, the Greeks
	Were to meet with disaster?
Poseidon	This change of heart is difficult to understand.

8

	Are love and hate so close in their extremes?
Athene	Have you not heard that my temple was defiled,
	That Ajax came and dragged Cassandra out,
	While the Greeks, so very proud of what they call
	Their triumph, stood smugly by and did not say a word?
Poseidon	Even thought it was *you* who conquered Troy for them?
Athene	Yes, and for this I need to see them suffer!
Poseidon	Poseidon would gladly help, if he but knew
	What he was being asked.
Athene	I ask you to destroy them.
Poseidon	Here in the harbour, or when they are out at sea?
Athene	When they break sail, Zeus himself will black out the sky
	With rain, and sleet, and hail, and roaring winds –
	His thunderbolt he has promised me 99
	To strike them down and set their ships ablaze.
	And you, Poseidon, the Aegean is yours;
	Whip the waves up into foaming mountain peaks,
	And glut the waters of each little bay
	With the bodies of their drowned. The Greeks must learn
	To hold the gods in awe, and reverence their shrines.
Poseidon	You need say no more, Athene.
	The Aegean will shudder under my grasp;
	And floating bodies knock against each cliff,
	Or else lie littering the sand for gulls
	To pick at. Return now to Olympus,
	Take the thunderbolt of god into your hands, and watch
	For when this proud fleet sets its sails towards the sea.
	Athene goes.

9

A mortal must be mad even to dare
To destroy a city, its temples and its tombs,
To violate the holy places of the dead,
When his own death is certain,
And stalks him so close.

*Poseidon goes. Hecuba is seen lying on the ground. Day
is dawning.*

Hecuba   Up wretch.
                    Head
                             off the ground.
Shoulders
              now,
                    ah.
This is no longer Troy.
Troy is gone, we but endure.   120
Fortune is a fickle wind,
So sail with that wind.
Turn the prow
Of this life's ship, and be swamped
In the wild waves of grief and of disaster.
Ah!
Yet what greater grief could woman bear?
Country, husband, children – lost.
The towering glory of a race all gone.
Was it all nothing, that nothing should remain?

How can this be lamented?
Yet how can I not lament?
Must I lie for ever on these stones.
My bony back racked with pain,
My head, my eyes, my ears
Throbbing with the rhythm of a torment
That would make my body writhe,
Rolling in time to the pulsing of my heart,
To the sound of tears, a dirge   140
To which no feet could dance.

Your swift ships came from Greece,
Their greedy oars clawing
At the wine-dark waters of the sea.

The piercing fife, and your trumpets,
Blared in bestial triumph
As you landed on the coast of Troy.

You came for that whore of Sparta,
Menelaus' loathsome wife,
Who caused the death of Priam
And all his fifty sons;
Helen, who wrecked unhappy Hecuba
Upon this reef of ruin.

A prisoner. Homeless. An exile.
Set to work as a slave.
An old, grey, plundered, mourning woman.
Enough! You –
You widowed wives of the warriors of Troy!
Brides, mothers and daughters of Disaster,
Come, Troy is burning, let us weep for Troy! 160
Once, with Priam's sceptre in my hand,
I would lead the dancers in the temple;
My voice rang out in joy and in praise,
Now it can but wail in lamentation!

Enter the women of Troy, the Chorus.

Chorus   Such a cry!
                    Hecuba, what has happened?
         We were in our tents
                              Fearful of the slavery
         That awaits us
                    When we heard you call out
         So piteously
                    And our hearts were seized with fear.
Hecuba   The ships are waiting in the harbour, my chil-
             dren.
         The sailors are ready at their oars.
Chorus   What is going to happen to us, Hecuba?
         Are they going to take us away?
         Will we never come back?
Hecuba   I do not know. I can but fear.
Chorus   O wretched women of Troy, the Greeks will
             come

11

	And 'Out of those tents, you slaves', they will call,
	'The ships are ready to sail', and all –
Hecuba	No! No, not all. Not Cassandra.[2] For pity
	Do not let them bring Cassandra here.
	They have driven her out of her mind; 180
	It is enough. Let them not shame her here.
	Spare me that, you gods, spare me that!
	Troy, poor Troy, you are finished.
	The living must now be dragged
	From the arms of the dead.
Chorus	Hecuba, are they going to kill us?
	We came running from Agamemnon's tents.
	We were afraid.
	Tell us what to do.
	What will become of us?
Hecuba	Be brave, my child.
Chorus	Is the steersman standing at the helm?
Hecuba	I do not know. I have been here since the dawn.
Chorus	Terror shudders in my heart.
	Has there been
	No word?
	What cruel tyrant must I serve as slave?
Hecuba	You will know soon. Soon we will all know.
Chorus	Will they carry me away to Argos,
	Phthia, or to some strange island
	In a foreign sea,
	Sad and far from my native Troy?
Hecuba	Oh where, when, and to whom must I go?
	A pale shadow of life, an ornament to death. 200
	What use is an old, grey woman as a slave?
	Will the Queen of Troy sit and watch their
	doors,
	And fondly nurse their murdering children?
Chorus	Tears cannot wash away her shame,[3]
	Nor pity mollify her grief.
	My fingers that followed the flying shuttle
	May be busy again, but not in Troy.
	They will not even let us see
	The graves of our dead sons.

Our fate is worse –
We are to be raped.
The curse of god strike the Greeks that night!

Must I draw water from the wells of Pirene,
And drudge as a common slave?
I have heard that Athens
Is a beautiful city,
Perhaps they will take us there.
But not to Sparta –
With its swirling river Eurotas –
The accursed home of Helen,   220
To be *her* slave.
To have to look at Menelaus,
Remembering what he did to Troy.
At the foot of Olympus, they say,
There is a country
Perfumed with flowers,
And rich with golden fruit;
If I cannot go
To Theseus' land,
I could wish to be taken there.
Or to Sicily –
Where under Mount Etna,
The mother of all mountains,
And guarding the straits of Phoenicia,
The Fire God hammers in his forge.
Once I heard a minstrel
Sing a song
About the brave men
Of that land.
The Ionian Sea   240
Sleeps in a little bay,
Where Crathis, fairest of rivers, flows
Through green, exultant fields,
Watering the tender roots of the flowers.
It is a magic river.
It strikes a yellow fire
Into men's hair.

13

It strengthens the warriors' limbs.
I might be happy there.

There is a herald coming from the camp.
They have reached their decision.
He looks in a hurry.
What will it be?
What will he say?
You see,
We are slaves already,
Waiting for orders.

Enter Talthybius attended by soldiers.

Talthybius	You know who I am, I think, Hecuba.
	This is not the first time that Talthybius
	Has been sent here as an emissary. 260
Hecuba	It has come, my daughters, the moment we most feared.
Talthybius	They've drawn lots for you if that's what you're afraid of.
Hecuba	Is it to be Thebes then,
	Or some city in Thessaly?
Talthybius	You will not all be staying together.
	Each one of you is destined for a different master.
Hecuba	Then tell who is going where, quickly.
Chorus	Tell us. Tell us.
Talthybius	One at a time.
Hecuba	Who drew
	Cassandra?
Talthybius	They didn't draw lots for Cassandra.
	Agamemnon selected her himself.
Hecuba	To serve the Queen of Sparta as a slave, poor child.
Talthybius	To be served in the king's bed more like it.
Hecuba	She is consecrated to Apollo.
	Her virginity is sacred! He knows that!
Talthybius	Perhaps that's why he wants her. Who can tell?
Hecuba	Then throw away your temple keys, my daughter,

	And scatter the holy garlands of the gods.
Talthybius	But it's an honour, the king's bed, surely?
Hecuba	And what has happened to my other daughter,
	That your men took away? Where is she? 280
Talthybius	(*hesitant*) Which one do you mean? Polyxena?
Hecuba	Yes.
	Which of your 'nobles' is she to be given to?
Talthybius	She has been assigned to Achilles' tomb.
Hecuba	Achilles' tomb? I don't understand you.
	What strange new custom of the Greeks is this?
	Is she some kind of functionary there?
Talthybius	She is at peace there, god rest her.[4]
Hecuba	Why do you say that? She is still alive?
Talthybius	You have no need to worry. Her troubles are over.
Hecuba	What of Hector's wife? My own brave Hector.
	Where will poor Andromache be taken?
Talthybius	It was agreed that Achilles' son should have her.
Hecuba	And me?
Talthybius	Odysseus, King of Ithaca.
Hecuba	Ah! No, not him. Then tear your hair,
	And flay the nails into your living flesh!
	Slave to that impious, vile, unnatural, beast,
	Whose lying tongue twists every right to wrong,
	Each boasted friendship into murdering hate!
	Weep now, and mourn for me, my women. 299
	Fortune has flung me to the bottom of her wheel,
	And I am ruined.
Chorus	Your fate is known,
	But ours is still uncertain, and that gives cause for fear.
Talthybius	You there, go and fetch Cassandra out. Come on, move,
	The general is waiting for her.
	We can deal with the others later.
	What was that? That light? What's happening over there?
	They can't be setting fire to their tents!
	Would you rather burn yourselves to death
	Than be taken away? Is freedom so dear,

The yoke of slavery so hard to bear?
A noble thought, but get those women out.
We will be held responsible for this!

Hecuba No. No, you are wrong. It is Cassandra;
The torch of prophecy is in her hand!

Enter Cassandra with a blazing torch in her hand.

Cassandra Hurl it high[5]
the light in my
hand. Oh, I
bring
FIRE
to the holy temple   320
blaze of worship, see.
See,
    Hymen,
        my king,
bridegroom of the blessed most blest.
King.
    Royal.
        Rape.
Oh to lie with,
        lie,
lying,
    lies.
Ah, mother, you weep
for my dead father,
mother in mourning,
lost with your country
        in tears.
Do not cry
    at my
        wedding,
the torch
    must blaze out
in a wedding brill –
iance
    Bright
as the virgin stars
at their dazzling death;

16

a virgin death
and my father dead
oh dance
     dance
for my dead father,   340
he too is blest.
Once I danced
for whom did I dance?
Apollo, was it you
         you
           YOU?
Ah the joy,
        the holy joy,
the laurels
      on the altar
in the temple
       and we
SANG–
Keep time with me, mother –
            in a whirling maze –
as you love me, mother,
Sing.
   Dance, I say,
greet the bride
      and wish her joy.
Your prettiest dresses, ladies.
Honour him
     who will dishonour me.

Chorus   She is out of her mind. Stop her, stop her,
Before she goes dancing down to the Greeks.

Hecuba   Let me hold the torch, child. You're too upset.
Look, it's not straight. Here, someone take it!
O god of fire, our wedding feasts once welcomed
   you,   360
Why bring this melancholy flame to mock our
   grief?
Misfortune brings wisdom, they say, but not to
   you,
My poor Cassandra. I had such hopes.
Little did I think that swords and spears

17

Would escort you to your bridal bed.
Our salt tears only can answer your song.

Cassandra Mother, be glad for me. Put flowers in my hair.
The man I am to marry is a king,
So take me to him. And, if I should hesitate,
Then you must make me go, for, as Apollo lives,
The great Agamemnon will find in me
A bride even more deadly than Helen.[6]
I am going to kill him; destroy his family
As he did mine; avenge my brothers' blood
And – but I must not speak of this,
Of the cold axe cutting into my throat –
And others' too – a mother butchered by her son,
The royal house of Atreus overthrown:
The bloody fruits of my enforced bed.
Yes, I know that I am mad, but listen,   380
For the words I speak are not my own.
Let me show you how this city of ours,
Even in ruins, is more blessed than the Greeks'.
One woman, one woman and her lust,
Sent their armies hunting after Helen,
Sent ten thousand soldiers to their death;
And their general, a man the world thought
    wise,
For the sake of what he hated most
Destroyed what he most loved, his own dear
    child,
His daughter; sacrificed her for his brother's
    wife;
To get back a woman whose adultery
Was of her own free will. No force was used,
    remember.
And when they came to the banks of Scamander
They died, day after day, they died. And why?
No armies threatened their shores, besieged their
    cities.
Far from their wives and from their children
No gentle hands prepared them for their graves;
The alien soil enclosed them where they fell.
While in their homes the sorrow was the same:

18

Old men in empty houses waited for dead sons;
Widows wept alone, and children trembled   401
In the barren beds of strangers. Weeds grew on
  graves.
Such was the glorious victory they won,
By deeds that earned them an unending shame!
And the Trojans? What fame could be more
  glorious
Than theirs? They died for their own country;
Carried home by their comrades to loving hands
That would take them and wrap them in their
  shrouds,
Lay them to rest in the land of their birth.
Each night those who returned slept in their own
  homes,
But there was no such comfort for the Greeks.

Hector's death was grievous to you, mother.
No, but hear me. Did he not die like a hero?
And how could this have been if the Greeks had
  not come?
Without them his fame would be unknown!
And Paris too married the daughter of Zeus.

The wise man does not look for war, but if it
  comes
Then he fights, like a hero, and if he dies
His death brings glory to his people.
So do not weep for Troy. And do not weep for
  me.   420
We need feel no shame. And I *know* my marriage
Will bring but further ruin to the Greeks.

Talthybius And if *I* did not know you'd lost your reason
I'd have you punished for this, calling down
  curses
On our generals just when they're about to sail.
She is right though; the great ones, who seem so
  very wise,
Are often no better than the rank and file.
Our king, the most powerful man in Greece,
Could have had any of these women he wanted,

19

Yet he chooses one that's out of her mind.
I wouldn't if I'd been in his place, I know.

But we can't very well punish you
When you don't know what you're saying.
Let's pretend the wind blew your words away
And I didn't hear what you said about Greece.
Come on, down to the ships with me now,
The general's waiting for his lovely bride.
And you be ready to follow, Hecuba,
As soon as Odysseus sends for you.
His wife is a good woman, they tell me,   440
You could do worse than be her servant.

Cassandra Servant? And what sort of servant are you?
Why is the name of herald so revered,[7]
When the creatures themselves are so vile?
Mere tools of state, everyone detests them.

So my mother is to serve Odysseus?
Then what of the oracle of Apollo
Which clearly says that she will die in Troy?

And Odysseus, the fool, he does not know —
And I must not tell;
                    silence lips,
                         sh!
Soon my sorrow, and all the miseries of Troy
Will seem to him like a golden summer's day.
Ten long years he has wasted here, and ten years
     more
Must wearily roll by, before at last and alone
He reaches his home.[8] Charybdis will strike
At him; Cyclops stride over the hills
Hungry for flesh; Circe bewitch his sailors
Into swine; the tall ships founder in the sea;
Temptations he must endure, and the holy cattle
Of the sun, slaughtered, will cry out with human
     tongues,   460
Prophesy his terror and the quick pain;
Alive into the deeps of hell he must descend
To find then —

                        that Sorrow has sped on before
And in Ithaca is waiting his return.
But why list his labours one by one?
                                    Quick!
Let us not waste time. Marry and murder.
Let a bed
            be prepared
In the house
                of the dead.
Oh, Agamemnon is a proud king.
Great and proud, is he not, Talthybius?
And what splendours still to come!
Hastily buried in the ground
In the middle of the night!
But what is that?
                    Nearby.
                            Down there.
                                        See.
At the foot of the cliff.
                        Naked.
In the stream.
                Winter water
                            washing over it.
So cold
            and white.
                        And the wild beasts
Thin too
            and hungry,
                        looking for food.
Their fangs have found it now
                            and are tearing
                                        sharp –
And it is I,
            Cassandra,   480
The virgin priestess of Apollo!
The garlands of my beloved god,
The wreaths of mystery I fling away!
They are gone
                out of my mind
With the rites of the temple.

21

Go,
   leave my body
         before it is made foul.
Oh, take them you pure winds
Sweetly now carry them
            back,
Back to Apollo.
Where is the ship? Show me where I must
   embark.
Quickly now. The wind is in our favour.
One of the three
        furies
           will go with you
On the sea.
        Goodbye, mother. Do not weep.
Goodbye, my city. My brothers under the
   ground,
And my father too. I will be with you soon.
You need only wait a little while.
And I will come.
        I will come as a hero,
Leaving behind me the royal house
Of Atreus
      wrecked
         ruined
           and destroyed!

Talthybius takes Cassandra out. Hecuba collapses.

Chorus Look, quickly, the Queen has fallen. Help her.
She does not seem able to speak. What shall
   we do?   502
Lift her up. We cannot leave her lying here.
Hecuba No, leave me alone, my children. Let me lie
Where I have fallen. Nothing is so unkind
As unwanted kindness.
I would call on the gods,
But they do not help. And yet suffering
Still turns the mind towards them. Sometimes I
   try
To recall the happiness we once knew. But

22

To do so only deepens the disasters of today.

I was of royal birth, and married
Into a royal house. I bore my husband sons,
Many sons. No woman in Troy, or Greece,
Or in the wide, green world could boast such
    sons –
And I saw them all killed, in battle against the
    Greeks.
I cut off my hair and laid it on their graves.
And when their father died – no herald came
To tell me of his death, and let my tears
Be shed in privacy; no, for he died   519
Before my eyes. I was made to stand and watch
While he was slaughtered at the altar.
The city was taken, and my daughters,
Whom I had nursed to give to noble husbands,
Were snatched from my arms and given to
    Greeks.
I will not see them again, nor they me.

And now the final degradation comes;
A crown of grief my old grey head can scarcely
    bear:
Slavery. Mine will be the wretched tasks
That wrack old age the most. To stand in the
    draught
By a heavy door – opening and closing –
A keeper of keys – the mother of Hector
Baking their bread, and nowhere to lay
My tired limbs but the rough stone floor – I
Who have known the silken beds of palaces.
Torn rags I will have to wrap around me
To mock my former dignity. And all this
Through woman's beauty and a young man's
    lust.
Cassandra, who shared the secrets of the gods,
Must pay the price now with her purity.
And Polyxena? What has become of her?   540
Not a son or daughter left to help me.
Why then would you lift me up? What hope is there?

23

THE TROJAN WOMEN

I once walked proudly through this city,
But drag me now to its furthest ditch
And throw me where the beggars sleep on stones,
There let tears choke the life from my heart!
No man, this side of death, can be called happy.

Chorus
A song,[9]
A new song,
O queen of song,
We would sing, but the sound
Dies on our lips.
Move thou the sweet melody of thy wings
Within our minds;
Inspire us:
With a strange song
Of sorrow,
And with the sound of tears,
To be wept
Into the grave of Troy;   560
Of the fall of Troy it must tell, and
Of the great horse brought to our gates
That brought us bloodshed and captivity.
Harnessed with gold,
Majestic and high
It stood.
But from deep inside
Came the rattle of armour,
As the rumbling wheels rolled
And it was pulled into the city.
On the Great Rock of Troy
The people stood shouting,
'The war is over!
Peace at last.
Go down,
Fetch this new idol
Safe to the temple
Of Pallas Athene
And there let it honour
The daughter of Zeus.'   580
Who in our city would linger behind?

24

When every young girl,
And old men too,
Came running from their houses
Singing with joy –
Eager to lay hands
On that engine of death.

The gates were glutted by a flood of feet;
Priam himself ran with the people
To honour the god,
By offering up
That cunning beast
Carved from a mountain pine.

While Argive soldiers crouched
Inside the womb of Troy's destruction.

Hauling on ropes of twisted flax
The crowd drew it along,
As though it were the hull of some black ship
They were launching on the water.

And at length it was brought to the temple,
And set upon the floor;   601
The temple of Pallas –
The white floor,
Which was to receive our blood.

Darkness fell.
The people were tired and happy.
Libyan flutes were heard
And the songs of Troy;
The voices of girls as they danced
Light in heart and gay;
Torchlight flickered against the blue,
Glowed from the windows of the town.
I was among the·dancers
Singing in the temple
Of Artemis-of-the-hills,
When suddenly the city rang
With a cry of terror,
The fierce scream of death.

Children clutched at their mothers' skirts.
War strode from his lair.   620
Trojans died,
By their altars,
In their homes,
In their beds;
Throats were cut,
And widows raped;
The shame and agony of Troy.

Andromache enters in a cart. She is holding Astyanax in her arms. Hector's armour and weapons are also in the cart.

Chorus   Hecuba, look, Andromache is coming.[10]
With Astyanax in her arms –
The Greeks have put them in a cart – Hector's
    sweet child.
Where are you going, Andromache?
And with Hector's armour too?
Are these to be trophies for Achilles' son?

Andromache   I am going wherever I am taken.

Hecuba   Ah, my children.

Andromache   You have no children now.

Hecuba   Aiai!

Andromache   Nothing remains –

Hecuba   But ruin, grief and torment
Beneath the debris of our pain.

Andromache   The gods hate us, and have since Paris was born;
Born, it seems, to destroy his country
For a woman's sake; born to watch vultures   640
Wheeling over the bodies of his friends;
Born to turn his sisters into slaves.

Hecuba   Ah, my children.

Andromache   But do not forget
That you are the mother of Hector too,
At whose hands unnumbered Greeks were slain.

Hecuba   I see only the hand of god,
Exalting brutish beasts,
And tumbling the mighty from their thrones.

Andromache   Aye, nobility enslaved; my son and I,

26

Like spoils of war, loaded onto a cart
And trundled away.

Hecuba   Already the soldiers
Have been for Cassandra. They took her by
    force.

Andromache Poor child. But you have other sorrows still.

Hecuba Others? How can one tell? Countless they come,
Each one a phœnix in the ashes of the last!

Andromache Polyxena is dead – An offering
At Achilles' tomb – They sacrificed her.

Hecuba That is what he meant – Talthybius!
Pitiful heaven, it is too plain now!

Andromache I saw it myself. I covered her   660
With my cloak, and said what prayers I could.

Hecuba Murderers! Polyxena. Oh, horrible!

Andromache She is dead. But to die, even as she died,
Is better than to live as we do now.

Hecuba No, child, no. Death is empty. In death
There is nothing; in life there is always hope.

Andromache Mother, mother, listen to me.
Face the truth and let it calm your grief.
To die, I say, to be dead, is to be –
As though one had never been born at all;
Which is better far than a life of pain,
For the dead feel no pain, know no evil.
But once a man has tasted joy
The loss of it will send his wretched soul
Searching restlessly long winter days.
In death Polyxena becomes as one
Who has not entered life, and so the death
That we lament, for her does not exist;
No evil, no pity, and no pain.   679
Whereas I, who sought honour and reputation,
And achieved both, see now how I fall.
As Hector's wife, I had to ensure
That nothing I did endangered his good name.
There were times when I wanted to go out
Walking through the streets, or visit friends,
But I knew, if I did, the gossips' tongues would
    start,

27

And I stayed at home. Nor did I allow
Other women to carry tales to me.
I kept to my own thoughts. That was enough.
And, in this way, I learned to be calm,
And modest in the presence of my husband.
I knew in what things I ought to obey,
And when it were wiser to overrule him.

I tried so hard to be a blameless wife
That the Greeks heard about me in their camp,
And my reputation became my ruin.
For when I was captured, Achilles' son
Demanded me. And so now I must serve
In the home of my husband's murderers.
But how? If I seem to forget Hector,   700
They will say I am unfaithful to the dead;
And yet if I stay true to Hector,
It will only make my new lord hate me.
They say that one night is enough
To dispel a woman's hatred for a man.
But how can it be so? How can a woman
Forget one man in the arms of another?
Why, if you take a cart-horse from its mate
It will not pull in harness any more.
Yet these are brutes, men say, and have not
    reason.
O Hector, you were all the husband
I could ever want: so noble, and so wise;
So strong and brave. I came to you a virgin
From my father's house; all my maiden love
I gave to you, and you are dead.
You are dead, and I am to be sent to Greece,
A prisoner and a slave. Hecuba, can you not see?
You weep for Polyxena, but by her death
She has escaped the pain that I know now.
The hope you find in life is not for me.   720
Hope is a dream, and cannot ward away the
    truth.
My heart does not deceive me.

Chorus   In your words we hear

28

The baleful echo of our own misfortunes.

Hecuba I have never been on board a ship,
But, from pictures, and from stories I have
    heard,
I know, that when a squall blows up,
If sailors think that they can weather it,
Then they lose no time – one man up aloft
To take in sail, another struggling at the helm,
While others bale the water from the decks.
But when the sea comes rolling higher than the
    ship,
And the storm beats down upon them, then they
    yield,
Abandoning themselves to the overwhelming
    waves.
So too, in excessive sorrow, I am dumb.
I yield. I cannot speak.
The tempest of the gods submerges me.

My child, think no more of Hector.
Tears cannot help him. Honour your new
    master,
And let your own sweet ways win his heart
    towards you.   740
By doing so you will gain a happiness
We all can share. And my young grandson here
Will grow to be a man, and then, perhaps,
Your children's children may one day rebuild
    Troy.

Enter Talthybius.

Talthybius Andromache! I salute the wife of Hector.
Do not hate me for what I have to say.
It is not any of my doing;
I have been sent by the Greek commanders.
Andromache Tell me the worst – for worse it clearly is.
Talthybius They have decided that your son –
Andromache Is not to be allowed to go with me?
Talthybius He will go with no one.
Andromache You cannot leave him alone in these ruins!

29

Talthybius	How can I make it easier for you?
Andromache	Do not try. Just tell me what you have to say.
Talthybius	It has been decided that your son must die.
Andromache	No!
Talthybius	It was Odysseus – he persuaded the council.
Andromache	O god, this is more than I can bear. 758
Talthybius	He said we could not allow a hero's son to live.
Andromache	Then may his own son's life be struck down too.
Talthybius	The child is to be thrown from the walls of Troy.

He goes towards her.

No, lady, no. Let it happen this way.
You will see it is wiser in the end.
Let go the boy now. There is nothing you can do,
So bear grief, as you were born to bear it, nobly.
The city is gone and your husband is dead.
One woman cannot hope to fight against us.
So do not try. You are too weak.
Submit. There is no shame in that.
Resistance can but sharpen harsh necessity.
Should the officers hear you curse them
The child might be denied burial;
Say nothing, and you may be allowed
To put him into his grave yourself.
You will find they will be much kinder to you.

Andromache But he is my son! And is that *why* he must die?
Must a son inherit his father's enemies?
Why then, it is Hector's strength, which saved
   the lives
Of others, that puts you to your death, my child.
And we used to dream that you would rule all
   Asia.   780
Are you crying, even though you do not under-
   stand?
Your little hands cling to my dress,
And you nestle against me like a young bird
Cowering under its mother's wings.
But it is no use. Hector cannot come back
From the grave to save you. His dead hand
Cannot hold this spear. The might of Troy has
   fallen.

Fallen – and you must fall – hurled from those
  heights –
Head down – this head – on to the stones –
Mercilessly broken – and none to pity you.
So young in my arms – your skin so sweet and
  soft.
Was it for this that I bore you – gave you suck
At my breast, wrapped you in your little clothes,
Endured pain, and sat up weary nights
To watch and care for you when you were sick?

Come close to me. Put your arms round my neck.
There. Tighter still. And press your lips to mine.

Oh, this is foul and barbaric! Have you no
  shame?[11]
What has this child done that you should kill
  him?
Nothing. And you know that. Nothing! Has
  Greece gone mad?   800
What are you doing here? Can you still believe
That Helen is the daughter of Zeus?
Oh, she had many fathers, that one, but never
  Zeus!
Evil begat her upon Hate!
And Murder and Death and every monster bred
  on earth!
But never Zeus to curse mankind with her.
God strike blind the infernal butchery of her
  eyes!

Take him then. Take him.
Dash him to death if you must. Feast on his
  flesh.
The gods are destroying us, how can I save him?
Cover my face.
And fling me on to your ship.
Having lost my child
                      I must go to my wedding.

Talthybius Come on now, boy. Let go of your mother.

31

Will you come with me? We haven't got far to
  go.
Up there on the walls. See?
Get hold of him one of you!
He has to die! Those are our orders.
They'll have to get someone else.
I cannot do it. 820
A man would have to have no heart.

The soldiers drag the boy away.

Hecuba A little boy. The child of my poor son.
Stolen from us. Torn from our arms. To be
  thrown
To his death. And what can I do?
Beat my breast and tear my hair. Nothing more.
There is nothing that I can do.
What sorrows have we been spared?
Are we not ruined utterly?

Andromache is taken away.

Chorus Far away,[12]
Over these waters,
The soft surf encircles
The island of Salamis,[13]
Where the ceaseless sound of bees is heard
Murmuring among the flowers.
It was Telamon, the king, ruled there.
And from his throne he would look
Across a little bay
To Athens' holy hill,
Where the goddess first bestowed on man
The green branch of the olive: 840
A shining crown from heaven
Which is now the glory of that city.
But Telamon left his island,
Sailed from the shores of Salamis,
Left that peaceful land,
And lent his strength in battle
To the warrior, Heracles;
Together they came,

And sacked the town of Troy.
Yes, once before,
In those far-off days,
Our city was destroyed by war.
For a vow had been broken:
Our king had promised him
Two matchless, white, immortal steeds,
But failed to keep his word.
For this
The armies of Greece set sail.
And at the mouth
Of our beautiful river Simois
They shipped their oars.
The canvas was furled.   860
The cables made fast.
And Heracles, the archer,
Brought on shore
His mighty bow,
And the arrows
Which the god's hand guided to their mark.
One shaft was bent at Laomedon's heart,
And the debt was paid.
But not content
They sent
The red breath of fire
Roaring over the walls,
Brought down the stones
Apollo's hands had laid.

Twice Troy has fallen.
Twice the fires have burned.
Twice the spears of Greece
Have gored into our sides.
In vain then Ganymede,[14]
Lost son of Laomedon,   880
Do you move with graceful step
Among the seats of the gods,
Pouring wine from your golden bowl
Into the cups of heaven;
In vain do you serve,

33

While the city that gave you birth
Is burned to the ground below.
Listen. Can you hear?
By the sea's side,
The sound of birds,
The lonely cry of the gull
Wailing the loss of its young?
Hear then and pity the cries of these women.
Know that their husbands and their sons are
    dead.
Gone are the marble pools
Wherein you bathed,
The fields, where you once ran and played,
Laid waste;
Yet Ganymede,   900
By the throne of god,
Still smiles,
Serene in the beauty of his youth,
As Priam's kingdom falls.

Love, O Love,
Once you came to Troy
And you sang;
And the sound rose
High to heaven,
Where all the gods heard
Your praise of Troy,
And they came
Down to earth for our love.

We do not speak against Zeus;
But how could the white-winged Dawn,
Whose light all mortals adore,
Shine this day on our fallen towers?

It was here that she found her love;
A prince of Troy
And she bore him away   920
In a coach of gold
Drawn by the stars,
Bore him away to the sky.

Tithonus fathered the children of Dawn
And glory shone on this town.

But Troy has now lost that enchantment,
That brought us once the love of the gods.

Enter Menelaus, attended by an armed guard.[15]

Menelaus   How bright the sun is today. Today.
After ten years of war, the day that I lay hands
On *her* again. My wife – Helen. And yet,
It was not so much for her that I came to Troy,
As men seem to think. No, it was for him:
To meet that honoured guest of mine again:
The traitor who stole her from my house!
And at last – praise be to the help of the almighty
    gods –
He has paid the penalty; the spears of Greece
Have seen to him, and his kingdom with him.
All that's left for me now is to collect –
The Whore of Sparta. That's what the soldiers
    call her   940
In the camp, and I can hardly bring myself
To speak her name, yet she was my wife once.
But now she is a prisoner, with the other women,
And the men who fought so bravely in this war
To get her back, have left it to me
To pass sentence of death upon her, or,
If I should decide not to have her executed here,
Then to take her back to Argos. And that
Is what I intend to do. She must not die in Troy.
No, she will go with me – to Greece – in my own
    ship.
But once there I'll hand her over to those
Whose sons did die at Troy, because of her.
The final satisfaction can be theirs.
You, and you, in there and fetch her out.
Drag her out! By the hair! Her hair, curse it.
As soon as the wind turns we'll put her on board.

Hecuba   O Zeus, upholder of the Earth, whose throne
    Earth is,

Thou who art beyond our understanding;
Who, or whatsoever thou art, O Zeus,
Whether natural and determined Law,   960
Or reasoning but immortal Mind,
Hear this my prayer, as you pass on your sound-
    less way
Guiding the deeds of men to Justice.

Menelaus   That's a strange way to call on the gods, woman.

Hecuba   Menelaus, if you are really going to kill her,
Then my blessing go with you, but you must do
    it now,
Before her looks so twist the strings of your heart
That they turn your mind; for her eyes are like
    armies,
And where her glances fall, there cities burn,
Until the dust of their ashes is blown
By her sighs. I know her, Menelaus,
And so do you. And all those who know her
    suffer.

Helen is brought out by the guards.

Helen   Menelaus, is this display of violence
Calculated to frighten me; your henchmen
Coming to haul me out? I can quite understand
That you may possibly hate me, but, even so,
There is one question that I would like to ask:
Have the Greeks decided what to do with me?
Am I to be allowed to live?

Menelaus   Your case
Was given no special consideration.   980
It was simply decided that I
Should be the one to pass sentence on you.

Helen   Will I be permitted then to argue my case
Against this decision? To prove
That any sentence would be unjust?

Menelaus   I came here to condemn you, not to argue with
    you.

Hecuba   Let her speak, Menelaus, you cannot let her die
Without a hearing. But you can let *me* speak
    against her.

36

You do not know the things she did in Troy.
When the story is complete, it will be enough
To justify her death. That she will not escape.

Menelaus If she has anything to say, then she may speak.
But it's for your sake I'm granting this,
Not hers, you understand, not hers.

Helen You look upon me as your enemy,
So what difference can it make
Whether my case is a sound one or not?
You may not even bother to reply.
All I can do is to try and guess
What charges you would bring against me 1000
If you did make a formal accusation,
And then to rebut them with indictments of my
  own.
The fault then is hers! Yes, Hecuba!
Catastrophe was born the day that she
Gave birth to Paris. And Priam, too,
He must share the blame; was he not warned
In his dream of a son who would set the mortal
  world
On fire and bring it crumbling into ashes?
But did he kill the child? No, he shrank in fear.
And the dream came true! It all came true.
Have you forgotten how it happened?
Paris was set to judge between three goddesses.
'Choose me,' said Pallas, 'and I will give you
Phrygian armies that will conquer Greece.'
'Choose me,' said Hera, 'and I will give you
Dominion from Asia to the western sea.'
'Choose me,' said Aphrodite, 'and I
Will give you Helen.'
Stop now, and think what would have happened,
What must, by logic and by right have hap-
  pened,   1020
If Aphrodite had not won her prize
And Paris his: Greece would have been
  conquered
By the armies of Asia, bloodshed and war
On *our* soil, our people enslaved and slaughtered.

37

And what prevented this but *my* downfall?
Yet I, who was bartered for my beauty,
Stand here condemned, who should be crowned
  with honours.
But do not think that I have forgotten
The question that you ask, and ask unceasingly:
Why did I leave your house?
There is no simple answer to that.
For when the creature that this woman spawned,
Paris, her son, Alexander, call him
What you will, when he arrived in Sparta,
There was a goddess walking at his side,
A divine, and most potent accomplice.
And yet it was then, my unworthy husband, that
  you chose
To set sail for Crete, leaving me alone
With him in the palace. Why? Why?
But in conscience I must ask myself   1040
What made me leave my country for a stranger.
Immortal powers were at work, I know.
So if you must have revenge, punish Aphrodite,
And show yourself more powerful than Zeus,
For he who rules the gods in heaven, is a slave
To her, yet I am beyond your forgiveness.

When Paris was dead and in his grave,
Then my love was no longer subject to the gods,
And I ought to have escaped from Troy, you say.
But that is what I tried to do.
The sentries on the wall will bear witness
That time and again they caught me with a rope
Letting myself down from the battlements.

Ask yourself now, Menelaus, would it be just
To kill me, when I have suffered so much
  already?
I was forced into marriage. And though my suf-
  fering
Saved Greece, the Greeks have not lessened my
  pain.
Do you think you are stronger than the gods,

Menelaus?

When even to think so is folly – remember.

Chorus   Hecuba, speak for your children and your
country!   1060

Hecuba, unweave the web of her pleading!

When a smooth tongue speaks from a false
heart

The righteous are afraid.

Hecuba   Yes, and I will speak too for those goddesses she
slanders.

Would Hera ever take such leave of her senses

As to sell Argos to the barbarians,

Or Pallas let Athens be enslaved by Troy?

And all because of some childish whim

That set them squabbling on a windy hillside

About a prize for beauty? No, never.

Why should Hera bother about beauty?

Was she hoping for a husband more noble than
Zeus?

And Athene, whose virginity is sacred,

Was she perhaps planning a marriage in heaven?

Oh do not try to cover up your sins

By pretending that the gods are fools;

Only a fool would believe you.

Then you claim – oh I beg you do not mock us
so –

You claim that Love herself went with my son

To visit Menelaus. She went with him,   1080

When she could have stayed quietly in heaven

And lifted up you, and your entire city,

If she had wished, and set you down in Troy.

No, my son was handsome, was he not?

One look at him and it was your own heart

That conjured up the likeness of Love.

Love! Must every passing fancy be labelled
'love'?

Love and lust, how those words chime aptly!

You saw him in the golden splendour of his
robes,

Rich with jewels from the east, and you

Were eaten with desire. What could the petty
    state,
That you were used to, hold for Helen
Against the promise of magnificence in Troy,
Where gold, you thought, flowed from the very
    fountains?
The halls of Menelaus could not contain your
    greed.
But you say it was against your will
That you went with Paris. Did you scream?
Did anyone in Sparta hear you call for help?
Yet Castor was there, and your other brother,
Both strong young men, and willing surely 1100
To defend the honour of a sister?

And then I remember at Troy itself,
When you arrived with the whole Argive pack
Baying at your heels, and the siege began,
Whenever you heard of a Greek victory
You would clap your hands and sing Menelaus'
    praises,
Just to torment my son, and remind him
That he had to fight a rival's claim
Upon your bed. But if the Trojans won,
Then Menelaus here was nothing.
You took good care to sail the way that Fortune
    blew.
You'd no more loyalty for one side than the
    other.
You speak too of trying to escape,
Letting yourself down from the walls on a rope,
As if Troy were a prison. But tell me this,
Was the prisoner ever caught twisting
That selfsame rope into a noose, or trying
How the edge of a sword might end her despair?
Like any noble woman would have done
Who truly loved the husband she had lost. 1120
Over and over again I pleaded with you to go.
'Leave us,' I said, 'my sons will find other wives.'
I even offered to help you escape,

To have you conducted in secret
To the Argive ships, anything
To put an end to the fighting between us.
But you would not have that. Oh no. And why?
Because you would not leave the luxury
You had become used to; your vanity
Needed to have men kneeling at your feet.
That, to you, was greatness.

                                        And now
You dress yourself up in fine clothes
And come out here to brave the light of day
At your husband's side. Have you no shame?
You would have done better
To come crawling through the dust,
Trembling, and in rags, your head shaved
To show some awareness of your sins.
Menelaus, I beg of you, let your verdict
Be worthy of your country and of yourself;   1140
Let her death serve as an example,
That women who betray their husbands must
    die.

Chorus Remember the honour of your royal house,
Let your justice be swift and severe.
The Trojans know you for a man of iron;
Do not let it be said in Greece
That a woman could melt your heart.

Menelaus I think as you do. No one forced her to go.
She was wilfully unfaithful.
And her imputations against the gods
Are blasphemous. Take her away.
You will be stoned to death;
And in that little moment, when you are dying,
You will pay for all these weary years of war.

Helen No, Menelaus, no. Don't kill me!
Look, on my knees, I implore you,
Do not blame me for what the gods have done.
Have mercy, Menelaus. Forgive me. Forgive me.

Hecuba Think of your friends who died because of her.
Do not betray their memory. *I* implore you, 1160
In the name of their wives and their children.

41

Menelaus Silence, woman! She is nothing to me now.
Take her to the harbour and put her on the ship.

Hecuba Not your ship, Menelaus. Do not let her sail with
you.

Menelaus Why not?

Hecuba   No man quite loses all his love.

Menelaus That surely must depend upon the woman?
But it will be as you wish. Some other ship then,
Not mine. And in Argos she will die
As she deserves. A shameful death
For a life of shame. And let it be a lesson
To all women. May they remember it,
And fear it in their hearts.

Menelaus goes out. The soldiers lead Helen away.

Chorus You[16]
Have destroyed us, god!
Betrayed us to the Greeks!
There was a temple in Troy
Where we honoured you;
Burnt incense;
Built altars;
Filled the air with the fragrant scent   1180
Of myrrh.
But now, holy Mount Ida –
Where the valleys are green
With ivy, smooth leaves,
Green stars dark in the valley,
Where rivers run fast,
Swollen with foam
From the melting snow –
Is deserted.
And the white mountain peaks
That border the rim of the world,
The holy glades
That catch the first rays
Of the morning sun,
Abandoned.
For God has destroyed us

42

And betrayed us to the Greeks!

Never again will we make sacrifice.
Never again will you hear the dancers
Sing long   1200
And far into the night.
Gone are the ikons
Graven with gold,
The twelve holy moons of Troy.
Our city is burning
                              burning
                                        burning!
God,
On your throne in heaven,

Do you no longer care?

The spirits of our dead husbands
Wander the world of the dead;
Their bodies unburied,
Their souls unsanctified.
And we must now wander the sea –
In a black ship;
Its banks of oars moving like wings,
Beat-
        ing down
                        on the waves.
At the gates of the city
Our children stand herded together,
Clutching their mothers' skirts;
Many are weeping   1220
And a little voice cries:
'Mother, I want to stay with you.
Don't let them take me
On to their ship!'

O god, I pray,
That when Menelaus' ship
Is far out at sea,
Your blazing thunderbolt
Falls down from heaven
And splits his deck into splinters of fire

43

Burning along the oars

THE TROJAN WOMEN

Burning along the oars
That would carry us from our homes!
That it falls while Helen
Sits holding her glass in her hands
Gazing at her face.
That it falls and burns them all!

May they never live to see Sparta,
Nor the bronze temple of Pitana,
For my fear
Is that he will forgive   1240
Her whose sins
Brought shame to Greece,
Brought blood
To the rivers of Troy.

Talthybius enters with soldiers carrying the body of Astyanax.

New sorrow has grown
From the seeds of your tears,
Unhappy women of Troy.
See, Astyanax is dead,
Flung from the tallest tower they could find
Still standing in the city.

Talthybius There's only one ship left now, Hecuba,
Bound for Phthia, with the rest of the trophies
They awarded to Achilles' son.
Neoptolemus himself has gone ahead,
And he has taken Andromache with him.
I went on board with her before they sailed.
It brought tears to my eyes
To hear the way she wept for her country,
And paid her last farewells to Hector's tomb.
She made me promise, Hecuba, to ask you   1260
To give the child some fitting burial.
And this bronze shield that belonged to Hector,
She would like you to bury it with him,
For we have no time to build
A proper tomb of cedar-wood or stone.
It's a fine shield. We Greeks remember it well.

44

It was a sight to fear on the battlefield.
She could not bear the thought of it
Displayed in her new husband's home.
It would have brought back bitter memories.

They would not let her stay behind
To bury the boy herself – and so –
She asked me – to be sure to lay him in your
    arms.
Have you anything left to cover him?
An old cloak perhaps, and a few wild flowers?
Now, as soon as you have laid him out,
We will help you to put him to rest.
Then we must go. So do not delay.
One thing I did for you. On the way here
I washed the body in the river, and cleaned 1280
The wounds a little. I thought you would like
    that.
We will go and dig the grave then.
If we all work together it will save time,
And we'll be able to sail for home that much
    quicker.

Hecuba Lay the shield there.

Talthybius and the soldiers leave.

Yes, bitter memories, but precious ones.[17]
Oh, you Greeks! Ignorant savages!
If only your swords were as dull as your wits!
Were you so frightened of this little boy
That you had to kill him? Were you afraid
That he might one day raise Troy up again?
Even though when Hector was alive
With an army of thousands at his side
We could not withstand you? A little child
You now see as a threat to your safety?
What strange, unreasoning cowardice is this?
Fear without cause is despicable in men.

Pitiful and unnecessary was your death,
Poor child. If you had grown to be a man,
You might have died fighting for your city, 1300

45

Having known the noble pride of youth,
The joy of marriage and that royal power
Which makes a man a god. Your death might
  then
Be said to have been happy – if happiness
Exists in this grey world. But, as it is,
Although you saw the treasures in your house,
You were not able to make use of them.
Oh, but what cruel usage has this city
Made of you. The curls your mother brushed
And combed are matted now with blood, and
  here
Where our lips planted kisses, the white bone
Mocks us through the ragged mouths of your
  wounds.
These little hands we thought so like
Your father's – limp and lifeless. And your poor
  lips;
Such pretty things they used to say. I remember
When you came into my room, and climbed on
  my bed
Saying, 'Grandmother, when the gods call you
To their great home, I will cut a lock
Of my hair and lay it on your grave,   1319
And then march past at the head of all my troops
To do you honour.' A promise you were not to
  keep.
Instead, it has been left to me,
An old, and homeless, childless woman
To bury you. Has all my love and care
Come to this? What, I wonder, will the poets
  say,
What epitaph will they inscribe upon your
  tomb?
'This child the Greeks slew in fear'?
Yes, Greece should be proud of that. My child,
Your father's lands and goods have all been
  taken.
Your only heritage is this great shield,
The shield that Hector wore upon his arm.

Here on the strap, see the marks where his hand
Gripped the leather, and where the sweat
    ran from his face.
As he leant against it in the forefront of the
    battle.
Let it guard you now in the ground below.

Come, let us use what few poor robes we still
    have left
To clothe his body. God knows there is not much
That we can do, but let us do it royally.

With wild limbs waving, and clutching after
    stars,
Fortune dances crazily away.   1340

Chorus We took these cloaks from off the Trojan dead
To wrap around the child.

Hecuba I had always hoped to bring you garlands
When you stood in triumph at the games,
Famous throughout Troy for your skill with the
    bow,
And for your horsemanship; not like this.
But nothing remains. Helen has robbed us
Of our riches, and you of your life.

Chorus He was our prince,
And our hearts would break to look on him.

Hecuba On your wedding day you would have worn
Such robes as would have made your sweet
    young bride
The proudest princess in the whole of Asia.
And must I cover your body with rags?
And you, too, beloved shield of Hector,
Here is a wreath for you; triumphant always,
You will not die, but go now into the grave
With this boy. It is an honour greater,
And more deserved than any Greek could gain.

Chorus The earth itself will weep   1360
When it receives this child.
Mother, we must sing
The song for the dead.

Hecuba Yes.

47

Chorus Of the sorrows that never
Will be forgotten.

They sing.

We bring white linen for your wounds,
White linen for your head,
With white linen we will bind you,
Heal the wounds where once you bled.

Hecuba These are words only! Here lies the truth!
What powers have we? We make poor physicians here.
Soon among the dead his father's hands will hold him.

Chorus We bow to your shade,
And beat the ground,
Beat the ground with our hands.

Hecuba Women of Troy!
Chorus   Hecuba, what is it?
We are here.
          See, we are all with you.

Hecuba In heaven
     they knew,
          the gods.
They knew this.
          Not just foreseen.   1380
No. Not predicted,
          but planned.
                    Schemed.
Contrived this!
          This is their will!
Misery and pain
          for me and for Troy.
A city set apart
          for their especial hatred.
And all this time we were saying prayers
To them
     at their altars
          offering sacrifices!
And in return we have become a legend;
A theme for poets

to embroider with their lies.
Would to god we had been engulfed
In darkness and forgotten.

Take the body to its grave.
He has his flowers.
The dead do not care how they are buried.
The pomp only panders
To the vanity of the living.

The body is carried out.

Chorus   At his birth men envied him.
More than this poor body
Was broken in that fall.

There are men up on the walls.
Look, there. With firebrands.   1400
They seem to be waiting;
Just standing still.
Oh, what is happening now?

Enter Talthybius.

Talthybius   Set it alight!
My men have been ordered to burn down
What is left of the city. As soon as that
Is done, then we sail. When you hear the trum-
       pets
I want you women to come down to the harbour.
Hecuba, I am sorry. Yes, for you
I am truly sorry, but Odysseus' men
Are here to fetch you. And you must go – now.

Hecuba   It has come
              this moment.
                       I feel my heart
Swell with the culmination of my grief.
To have to go
              with the sight of those flames
Burning into my eyes.
                       I must get up.
I must see it.
              Do not fail me now,

49

THE TROJAN WOMEN

My limbs.
      I must see my city.
Say farewell to her.
        In all Asia
There was not your equal, but your very name
Will now be burned into oblivion,   1420
And your people scattered over the earth
As slaves. O god. God!

But why should I call upon the gods?
Once before I called, but they did not come.
They did not listen.
              Women, hear me!
Follow me into the fire. Let us die
With our city in the fury of these flames!

Talthybius Stop her! Get a hold of her! Poor creature,
Her sorrows have sent her mad. Careful there.
Bind her if necessary. She belongs
To Odysseus now; we must not lose her.

Hecuba Son of Cronus, Lord of Phrygia,
Zeus, our father,
Do you see
How your children suffer?

Chorus He sees, but the city is burning;
Soon there will be no Troy.

Hecuba Flames are running
Over the roofs of the houses.

Chorus After the spears come the spikes of flame. 1440
And the smoke billows up on the wings of the
  wind.

Hecuba O, land that gave birth to my children,
O, children, hear me when I call to you.

Chorus Your children are dead, they do not hear.

Hecuba Then I kneel to their souls in heaven,
And beat the ground with my hands.

Chorus We too will kneel by your side,
For our dead husbands' sake.

Hecuba We are driven away –

Chorus   Away from our homes.

Hecuba To be sold as slaves.

50

O, Priam, are you dead,
And no friend left to bury you?
And do you know my fate?

Chorus Darkness has closed
Over his eyes.
Unholy murder
Put an end
To his most blessed life.

Hecuba O you temples of the holy gods.
After the spears come the spikes of flame.   1460

Chorus The ashes will blow
And all
    will be forgotten.
The dust and the smoke
Rise to heaven.
I cannot see.
The name will vanish from the land.
When the city is gone
Only sorrow remains.

The climax of a growing roar of fire. The citadel collapses with a great crash.

The citadel has fallen.

Hecuba Ruin . . . ruin.

Chorus The earth shook
And engulfed the city.

Hecuba Come, old limbs, lead me now.
Teach me to walk like a slave.

Chorus Farewell, my city. Farewell.
The ships are waiting
And we must go,
For dust and death
Are now the lords of Troy.

They leave. The trumpets sound from the Greek ships.

NOTES

1 The play opens with the customary prologue which sets the

NOTES

scene and explains the situation. Poseidon, the god of the sea, had favoured Troy, but Pallas Athene, a daughter of Zeus and a ruthless battle-goddess who had previously supported the Greeks, is now angry because of the sacrilege they have committed in her temple and so asks Poseidon to assist in her revenge by destroying the Greek fleet.

2 Cassandra, daughter of Priam and Hecuba, had been given the gift of prophecy by Apollo, who had fallen in love with her, but when she refused his love he turned that gift into a curse by ensuring that, although her predictions would always be true, no one would ever believe her; so, even when she knew what disasters were coming, she was always powerless to prevent them.

3 The chorus is a formal lament in which the women accept the inevitability of their fate. Notice that the women of Troy praise Athens. This may be seen as ironic, but Euripides was in no way disloyal to his country; he simply disapproved of what they had done in Melos.

4 Talthybius cannot bring himself to tell Hecuba that Polyxena has been sacrificed at Achilles' tomb. Although a member of the victorious army, he clearly has no stomach for the brutalities that are being carried out.

5 Cassandra's ravings are a bitter parody of a traditional wedding hymn.

6 Cassandra here foretells the fate of Agamemnon. He had sacrificed his daughter, Iphigeneia, in order to get a favourable wind for Troy. Ten years later he returned in triumph, but was murdered by his wife, Clytemnestra, who was in turn murdered by her son, Orestes. The story is told in Aeschylus' trilogy *The Oresteia*.

7 Heralds were under the protection of Hermes and were safe from attack. Their authority was normally unquestioned.

8 The predictions here form part of the story of Homer's *Odyssey*.

9 The chorus reflects Hecuba's grief and provides a woman's view of the fall of Troy.

10 Andromache had been the wife of Hector, the most famous of all the Trojan heroes. He had been killed by Achilles. Astyanax is their son. They represent the fate of the widows and children of a defeated nation.

NOTES

11   These lines can be taken as referring to the situation in Melos and are certainly a powerful element in Euripides' anti-war theme.

12   A lyrical chorus, but one of despair which tells the story of a previous fall of Troy. Heracles had undertaken to rescue a girl who was being sacrificed to appease a sea-monster. In return he asked for two horses that had belonged to Zeus. He killed the monster, but the Trojan king, Laomedon, refused to give up the horses, so Heracles killed him and, with his friend Telamon of Salamis, destroyed the city.

13   Salamis is claimed as the birthplace of Euripides, and he is said to have written his plays in a cave looking out over the sea.

14   Ganymede was a beautiful Trojan youth who had been carried off to Olympus by Zeus's eagle to become cupbearer to the gods. Likewise Tithonus (l. 920), another Trojan, was carried off by Aurora, the goddess of the dawn. The point here is that although the gods once loved the Trojans, they seem to have forsaken them now.

15   There is a distinct change in the emotional atmosphere of the play at this point. After so much pain and grief we see Menelaus, smug and pompous, and with an attitude that is shockingly casual. Then comes Helen, totally unrepentant, and having dressed up for the occasion – something that enrages Hecuba. The outcome of their debate is never in doubt: the audience knows from *The Odyssey* that Menelaus will not kill her. The dramatic significance of the scene is that this totally unheroic, squabbling couple have been the *cause* of all that suffering.

16   The Chorus sense that Menelaus will not take revenge on Helen, and the feeling of gloom and total defeat that they express prepares us for the coming of the soldiers with the body of Astyanax. His burial is the burial not only of what is past, but of all hope for the future.

17   There is real bitterness against the savagery of the Greeks in many of the lines in this speech by Hecuba, especially:

>   What epitaph will they inscribe upon your tomb?
>   'This child the Greeks slew in fear'?
>   Yes, Greece should be proud of that.

Helen

The Legend
The whole point of this play is that it does *not* tell the usual story of Helen of Troy. That had already been dealt with in *The Trojan Women*. For his plot this time, Euripides seems to have taken a lyric poem called the *Palinode*, written around 600 BC by Stesichorus. Stesichorus had previously written a poem in which he had said some very harsh things about Helen, and was struck blind as a punishment. He only regained his eyesight after he had written this Palinode, or 'apology', in which he said that Helen herself had never really gone to Troy at all, and that it was only a 'phantom' of her that was there. To this, Euripides added another suggestion made by Herodotus, that Paris did steal Helen, but bad weather drove his ships onto the coast of Egypt, where the king, Proteus, disapproving of the whole affair, sent him away again but kept Helen safely in his own palace to wait for her husband. Meanwhile, the Trojan War went on even though the Trojans were insisting, quite rightly, that they had not got Helen.

Euripides takes hints from both these sources, adds the idea that Hera made the phantom to spite Aphrodite, and has Hermes transport the real Helen to Egypt. To complicate matters, he introduces Proteus' son, Theoclymenus, a true barbarian who is set on marrying Helen himself. All that is then needed for the total comic confusion that Euripides is aiming at, is to have Menelaus shipwrecked off the coast of Egypt on his way back from Troy with the 'phantom' Helen that he thinks is really his wife.

The Play
Some writers on this play have been at pains to establish what kind of tragedy it is, but the answer must surely be that it is not a tragedy at all. It does not conform to any of the accepted patterns of tragedy. It does not treat, in a serious way, the downfall of a noble figure, nor does it inspire pity and terror. No one suffers. There is a happy ending. Helen is re-united with her husband, and there are a lot of laughs. Moreover, the laughs come because of ambiguities, confusions and misunderstandings, which are the

essence of comedy romance. For the world of comedy romance is a world where things are very rarely what they seem to be, and when this play opens there are two Helens, a real one and a phantom one; a major war has just been fought over the phantom, while the real one goes unrecognised. Helen's husband has a world-wide reputation as a hero, but when we see him, dressed in rags, he turns out to be a boaster and a bore, not very bright, and, without his army, something of a coward. The King of Egypt is no better, certainly no brighter, and his sister, a great prophetess, only manages to predict something that has just happened. It is therefore left to the Whore of Sparta – who proves, of course, to be a virtuous lady of great wit and charm – to organise her own rescue, and she does so with that stock-in-trade of all such romances: a feigned death.

Written in 412 BC, this is a light-hearted play with a complex and unlikely plot, some foolish characters, and choruses which seem to anticipate grand opera in being elegant and lyrical, but not always relevant.

Helen

CHARACTERS

Helen
Teucer   a Greek sailor
Chorus   of captive Spartan women
Menelaus   husband of Helen
Portress
Messenger   an old man, one of Menelaus' crew
Theonoe   a prophetess, sister of Theoclymenus
Theoclymenus   King of Egypt
Messenger   a servant of Theoclymenus
Servant   one of Theoclymenus' servants
Dioscuri   Castor and Pollux, Helen's brothers, sons of
                    Zeus and Leda, now gods

---

*Egypt, in front of the royal palace, near the mouth of the
Nile. To one side is the tomb of King Proteus, where
Helen has taken sanctuary.*

Helen   This mighty river is the nymph-blessed Nile.
No rain falls here, but high up in the hills,
When the white snows melt and the waters rise,
Great floods slake the dust of thirsty Egypt.

Proteus once was lord of this land;
He ruled it from his island throne on Pharos
With his bride, the sea-nymph Psamathe.
Two children they had; the elder, a son,
Whom his father – to honour the gods –
Named Theoclymenus, and a daughter,
The brightest jewel of her mother's life,
Who in her younger days was known as Eido,
But when she grew to womanhood and they
    found that

56

HELEN

Like Nereus, her grandfather,
She too was able to foretell the future,
They gave her a more fitting name – Theonoe.[1]

But my home – while no less famous – is not
In Egypt. It is Sparta. I am the daughter
Of Tyndareus, though legend has it
That Zeus, flying to earth in the likeness   20
Of a swan, was attacked by an eagle,
And sped for safety into the arms
Of Leda, my mother, only to show
His treacherous gratitude by an act of rape.
And that, if what they say is true,
Is how I was born. My name is Helen.
And the rest of my sad story? I shall tell you.
Three goddesses, Hera, Aphrodite,
And Pallas Athene, the daughter of Zeus,
Came to a wooded valley on Mount Ida
Where young Prince Paris lived, and demanded
His judgement: which of them was the most
    beautiful?
But Aphrodite cunningly made use
Of *my* beauty – if, that is, misfortune
Ever can be beautiful – she used me
As a bribe, and won the prize. So Paris
Left his flocks and came looking for me in
    Sparta.

But Hera, in high rage at having failed
To win the prize herself, blew such wishes
To the winds, and out of the air itself   40
Fashioned a living likeness of me.
And that – that was what she gave to Paris,
Poor fool, thinking he had captured me,
Yet holding nothing in his arms but Fantasy.

Zeus though had further heartaches for me still.
Greece and unhappy Troy he drenched with war
As if mankind were some foul infestation
He would wash away, and leave Achilles
In sole eminence. Trojans, or so they thought,

57

HELEN

Died for me on the spearheads of Greece,
But it was my name alone – only my name
They fought for. But Zeus did not desert me.
He sent Hermes, who came and caught me up
In folds of air, veiled me in clouds
And brought me here to the house of Proteus,
Whom the gods knew for a most upright man,
Who could be counted on to guard my honour
And keep me safe for Menelaus.
And here I am. But Menelaus himself –
Sadly, he gathered together an army   60
And went in warlike quest of me to Troy;
Where because of me the bodies of the slain
Litter the banks of the Scamander.
And all this I must endure; must hear myself
Denounced as disloyal to my lord
And cursed for having lit the fires of livid war!

Why then, you ask, do I go on living?
Because of a prophecy that Hermes made.
He said that when at last my husband learns
That I never was at Troy, never was
Untrue to him with any man, then once again
I shall return and live with him in Sparta.
Such was my hope, and while King Proteus
Lived, I had no fear; but now he's dead,
And Theoclymenus, his son, is set
To marry me. But I will keep faith
With my own lord, and so have come, as suppli-
    cant
To Proteus' tomb, that though my name
May be reviled in Greece, my honour may be
    safe.

*Enter Teucer, a Greek sailor. At first he does not see
Helen.*

Teucer A palace! And magnificent! Who can he be   80
Who commands such towers and battlements,
And walls that might well lap in wealth itself?

58

HELEN

He sees Helen.

But god, what's this? The odious image
Of that murderess witch who ruined me
And ravaged Greece. God's curse on you
For looking so like Helen. If I were not
On foreign soil I'd loose an arrow through you
    now,
Yes, just for looking like that child of Zeus!

Helen   No, wait, don't go, whoever you are.
Don't go blaming me for what another's done.[2]

Teucer   I am sorry. Anger took my tongue.
But there's not a Greek alive who does not loathe
That daughter of Zeus. I was wrong though.
    Forgive me.

Helen   But who are you? Where have you come from?

Teucer   I, lady, am one of those ill-fated Greeks.

Helen   Oh. Then it's no wonder you hate her.
But tell me your name, where your home is, your
    family.

Teucer   My name is Teucer. I come from Salamis.
I am one of Telamon's sons.

Helen   Then what brings you here to this valley of the
    Nile?   100

Teucer   I was driven out of Salamis – exiled.

Helen   How awful for you. Who was it drove you
    out?

Teucer   Telamon, my own father, and I thought he really
    cared for me.

Helen   But why? He must have had some reason.

Teucer   Because of the death of my brother Ajax at Troy.

Helen   How? You didn't kill him surely?

Teucer   No. He killed himself, with his own sword.

Helen   He must have been mad. No sane man could do
    such a thing.

Teucer   Have you ever heard of Achilles? Peleus' son?

Helen   He was one of Helen's suitors – or so I've been
    told.

Teucer   He was killed too and his friends quarrelled over
    his armour.

59

Helen	Yes, but how did all this affect your brother?
Teucer	Someone else won that armour and so he killed himself.³
Helen	And because of that, they exiled you?
Teucer	Yes, because I didn't die by his side.
Helen	I see. So you were at Troy yourself?
Teucer	I helped to destroy it and was myself brought down.
Helen	Destroyed? Is the city gone? Was it burned?
Teucer	There's not so much as the outline of its walls left now.
Helen	O Helen! How many Trojans must have died for you! 120
Teucer	Trojans? Greeks too! There was such slaughter done.
Helen	How long is it now since the city was burned?
Teucer	Seven years Time's scythe has harvested.
Helen	And before that how long were you there?
Teucer	Month after month ... years ... oh, ten years!
Helen	And was she captured in the end – Helen I mean?
Teucer	Yes. Menelaus hauled her off by her hair.
Helen	Did you see her, or is that just what you've been told?
Teucer	I saw her with my own eyes, as I see you now.
Helen	But might the gods not have tricked you with a dream?
Teucer	I really don't want to talk about this any more.
Helen	But do you believe all you saw?
Teucer	Lady, when I see something, I see it.
Helen	So Menelaus is at home now, with his wife?
Teucer	No, he's not – not in Argos, nor yet in Sparta.
Helen	There's something behind those words, isn't there? What?
Teucer	They say he's vanished, and his wife with him.
Helen	But didn't they all set sail together?
Teucer	Yes, they did, but the fleet was scattered by storms.
Helen	Where were they though? Where did all this happen? 140

HELEN

Teucer	Far out at sea, somewhere in the mid-Aegean.
Helen	And hasn't there been any sign of them since?
Teucer	Nothing at all. Rumour has it he's dead.
Helen	(*aside*) Dead! Oh, no.

And Thestia's daughter?

Teucer Do you mean Leda? Leda's dead; that I do
know.

Helen Her daughter's disgrace broke her heart, I
suppose.

Teucer So they say. She took a rope and hanged herself.

Helen And the two sons she had by Tyndareus – are
they still alive?[4]

Teucer Some say they are – some say they're not.

Helen But what am I to believe?

(*aside*) And what endure?

Teucer They're gods now, so one story has it, up among
the stars.

Helen Gods! That's wonderful! But what do the others
say?

Teucer That they took their own lives too – by the
sword;

That their sister's shame drove them to it.
But enough of this. I've grieved for it already.
I came here to find Theonoe
The prophetess. Will you take me to her?
I need her help for a fair wind to Cyprus,
That sea-rimmed isle Apollo said
That I should make my home, and re-name
Salamis   160
In honour of the land where I was born.

Helen Cyprus? The next high wave would wash you
there;

You need no guide. But you must get away,
And quick. Now. Flee before Theoclymenus
Sees you. He has gone out hunting with his
hounds
But any Greek that he lays hands upon
He kills. Don't ask me why. I cannot tell you.
Nor would it help you if I could.

Teucer For these kind words, lady, may the heavens

61

HELEN

Reward you. And to think that I took you
For Helen. You share her looks, but that is all.
Your hearts – oh, your hearts are nothing like.
I pray she never sees her home again.
But you, lady, my blessings go with you, always.

Teucer goes out.

Helen   Some sorrows fret their own laments,
But what new dirge could sound the depths
Of this great grief of mine?
What muse may I invoke to match   180
My misery and tears?

Come, you Daughters of Earth,
You sirens of the sea,
Stretch your wings and fly,
Here, now, to me.
Bring me your Libyan flutes,
Your harps, your pipes, your lyres,
And let your deathly music
Accord with my despair;
Let each note chime with my sorrow,
Let each note fall to my pain.
And if in the Halls of the Dead,
Persephone will blend
Her mournful songs with mine,
I shall for ever honour her
With libations from these eyes.[5]

Enter a Chorus of captive Spartan women.

Chorus   I was down by the river,
Spreading out purple robes
On the rushes
To dry in the glare of the sun,   200
When I heard my lady.

(individual voices)

She cried out.
Such a pitiful cry.
A cry of grief.

62

HELEN

And of pain.
Like the scream of a nymph
In an echoing cave
Caught
And raped by Pan.

Helen Wretched freight of that foreign fleet,
Daughters of Greece, O hear me.
A sailor has been
With a tale to bring
New tears to tearful eyes.
Troy is finished – burned!
Men without number
Have gone to their graves
Thinking they died in my name.
And Leda, my mother, has hanged herself   220
At the thought of my disgrace.
My lord, he says, was lost at sea.
And both my brothers too,
The glory of their race,
Have left this sorrowing earth;
Have left the fields by the river Eurotas
Where they once rode and ran,
Drear and desolate.

Chorus Weep for the fate of Helen:
And a life that can be no life;
A life that began
When a great white
Snowbloom of swan's wing,
The bright seed of Zeus,
Burst in your mother's womb.
What griefs have you not felt?
What pains have you not known?
Leda and both your brothers dead,
And you quite tearblind
For a glimpse of home –   240
Yet a home
Where every common gossip
Thinks you wanton in a heathen's bed.
And now if your own true lord
Has perished too,

63

HELEN

I fear you never will again
Grace your father's house
Or Athene's temple of Bronze

Helen Who was it felled the tree
That brought us all such tears,
The tree they shaped
To form the keel
Of the accursed ship
That brought the son of Priam
And all his brutish crew
To sue for me in Sparta
And wreck my life with his love?
Yes, and who came with him?
Who but Aphrodite? That cruel,
That treacherous, that murderous   260
Goddess of love
Who brought death
To Trojan and Greek alike.

But Hera, who shares the throne of Zeus
On the golden heights of heaven,
Sent the fleet-footed Hermes down
To where I walked gathering roses
Laying them gently in the folds of my dress
To take to Athene in her temple;
And he snatched me up in his arms,
And flew with me through the sky
Here to this wretched land;
While in Troy,
On the banks of the river Simois,
Where the Greeks did battle
With the princes of Priam,
All men cursed my name;
But not one of them knew
That they fought and fell
Not for me but a phantom.

Chorus We know you have good cause for sorrow,   280
But the burdens of life must be borne.

Helen Borne? Good friends, I am weighed down by
their weight!

64

HELEN

Was not my birth itself a monstrous omen?
What other woman in the world was born
From an egg, as Leda, they say, bore me?
And hasn't the whole course of my life
Been monstrous since, either through Hera's
    doing
Or through what they call my beauty? Beauty!
Oh, if only my face were like some picture
That could be wiped clean and done again,
Repainted to make me look plain.
Then the people of Greece might cease to speak
    ill
Of my name and remember some good I have
    done.

If a man feels that the gods have dealt him
One bad stroke of luck, that in itself is enough;
It's sad, but a single blow may be endured.
Me, they have overwhelmed with woes.
Firstly, though innocent, I am reviled;
And if a true guilt is hard to live with,
It is insupportable when undeserved.   300
Then the gods snatched me from my home
And left me friendless in this alien land:
A freeborn woman to become a slave
Among barbarians; for in a barbarous land
No one but their savage ruler can be free.
But still my hope had one strong anchor left:
That Menelaus would someday rescue me.
But now he's dead, that anchor's gone.
My mother too – and I must hear myself
Unjustly held to be the cause of all.
My daughter – the pride of all our house,
And my great joy, a woman now, and still
    unwed.
And my two brothers, the sons of Zeus, both
    dead.

Nothing but disaster, undeserved! Yet no
    misdeed

65

HELEN

Of mine, misfortune only was its root.
And now I alone am alive – yet dead too,
For if I were to reach my home they'd shut
    me
In their deepest dungeon, believing me
To be that Helen Menelaus sought
In Troy. Oh, if only Menelaus   320
Had lived, he would have known my body's
    truth.
But it is over now. He's dead, I know.
And yet I keep on living. And for what?
Will another marriage rid me of these ills?
Life with a barbarian? Sharing the pomp
Of his court? No, when a woman lives
With a man she loathes, she learns to loathe
Her own self too. Better to die. But how?
Our very slaves hold it shameful to hang.
I could never do that. But a sharp knife
Has some touch of honour in it, and death
Comes in an instant. And is this what I
Am brought to? For some women their beauty
Is their glory – for me it was my ruin.

Chorus	But Helen, whoever he was, this Greek,
	Can you be sure he was telling the truth?
Helen	He told me plainly that my lord was dead.
Chorus	Yes, and a false tale can be all too plain.
Helen	But never with that ring of simple truth.
Chorus	You're always so ready to fear the worst. 340
Helen	Fear enfolds me, drives me to what I most dread.
Chorus	How many in the palace can you count on as
	your friends?
Helen	Why all of them – except the one who wants to
	marry me!
Chorus	Then listen – I think you ought to leave this
	tomb...
Helen	Do you know what you're saying? Leave the
	safety...
Chorus	(*individual voices*)
	Yes, go into the house; find Theonoe,
	Wisest daughter of the Nereids.

HELEN

She knows and understands all manner of
things.
Ask her if your husband is alive or dead.
And then – when you are really certain –
Then will be the time for you to laugh or
mourn.
What use is grief when nothing's known for
sure?
Do as we say. Go. Leave the tomb.
Talk to Theonoe and then you'll know.
What are you waiting for? There in the palace
Is a friend who can put your mind at rest.
I'll come with you if you like.

                    I'll ask her.
She needs a woman's help.

                    We'll go together.

Helen   You're right, my friends, I'll do it.
Into the palace now, quickly.   360
And there we will learn
What the future has in store.

Chorus We will do whatever you ask.

Helen   It frightens me though.
This is a truly fateful day.
Somewhere a word has been written,
And we may read it through our tears.

Chorus Don't weep too soon.
Meet grief as it comes.

Helen   But what of my husband?
Is he alive?
Do his eyes
Still see the chariot of the sun
Blaze across the skies,
The circuit of the stars?
Or has black death
Enshrouded him
In its own dark deeps?

Chorus Hold hard onto hope,
Whatever is to come.   380

Helen   You spirits who sing
In the reeds

67

HELEN

	Of the holy river Eurotas,	
	I call on you	
	And swear	
	That if this tale is true,	
	That if my lord is dead...	
Chorus	What wild words are these?	
	What are you saying?	
Helen	A knot I'll noose	

    Round my own neck,
Cut my own throat,
Or plunge a knife
Deep in this breast
Until my very life floods out
In bloody sacrifice
To those dire goddesses,
And to that son of Priam
Who walked his herds
On the slopes of Ida   400
Long, long ago.

Chorus If only some god would smile on you now
And drive these ills away.

Helen

Weep now,
Oh, weep for Troy,
Bowed down so low,
So pitifully low,
By no deeds of her own.
I was her gift
From Aphrodite,
But with me I brought pain,
Rivers of blood and tears;
Grief to those who already mourned
And anguish to those who grieved.

Mothers weep for their sons in Troy
And sisters
Tear their hair
On the banks of the river Scamander
Where their brothers died.
In Hellas too,   420
The land of the Greeks,

HELEN

The same lament is heard;
And tears run red down women's cheeks
That their own nails have clawed.

I have heard
That sometimes
Sorrows much like mine
Miraculously turned to joy:
That Callisto
Raped by Zeus in Arcady
Was changed into a bear. [6]
A kinder fate
Than my poor mother knew,
For then the gentle look
In her brown eyes
Showed human troubles laid aside.
And Artemis,
Jealous of the beauty
Of Merops' daughter,
Drove her from her company,   440
Turning her into a winsome doe
With little golden horns.
But the beauty I was cursed with
Brought grief to Greece
And burnt Troy to the ground.

*Helen and the Chorus go into the palace. After a few
moments Menelaus enters. He is dressed in rags.*

Menelaus   I really am beginning to think
That it might have been far better
If I never had been born at all.
If my grandfather – Pelops his name was,
The one who won that chariot race
Against Oenomaus at Pisa –
If, when his father put him in that stew
And tried to serve him up to the gods,
That they'd actually eaten him!
He'd never have sired my father then.
That was Atreus. Yes, he was my father,
Married Aerope, and they had us:

69

HELEN

Agamemnon and Menelaus,
The world-famous brothers who led the attack
On Troy! [7] Led? Well, I don't want you to think
I'm boasting, but I was the real leader.   462
It's far more than just a question of rank;
Those men followed me because they loved me.
We did suffer some quite heavy losses, true;
It was unavoidable. Happily though,
There were plenty of others got home safely
To tell their loved ones how those heroes died;
But me – I've been wandering the wild
Grey waves ever since the day Troy fell,
Trying to get home, but the gods won't let me.
I must have sailed down every bleak and pitiless
Backwater on the coast of Libya,
But every time I got near home some wind
Rose to blow me out to sea again
With never a landward breeze to fill my sails.
And now I'm cast up here; my friends all lost;
My ship shattered into a thousand pieces
On the rocks; only the keel held out,
And that – but how I'll never know – was what
    saved us,
And we got ashore – myself and Helen   480
Whom I saved from Troy. I've no idea
Where we are, or what kind of people live here.
I could have asked. I did see some people,
But dressed like this, I was too embarrassed to.
It's hardly decent, so I kept out of their way.
Falling on hard times, a great man
Is bound to feel it more than those who are used
    to it.
To tell you the truth, I'm quite exhausted.
I don't know when I last had anything to eat.
And these rags are all I could lay my hands on.
Usually I'm dressed quite splendidly,
But all my clothes went down with the ship.
My wife though – the cause of it all – she's safe.
I've left her hidden down there in a cave.
The other survivors are guarding her

70

HELEN

While I've come up by myself to try and find
Some supplies to take back to them.
I noticed these battlements and that's why I'm
    here.
It's an impressive entrance. He must be rich.
He'll be able to help us. Well there's no point
Begging from the poor; they'd be no use.   501
Hello there! Gatekeeper! Would you mind
    coming here.
I've got a message for your lord. I need help.

*The palace door opens, and the Portress, quite an old
lady, appears.*[8]

Portress	Who's that? What do you think you're doing
	Hanging around these gates? Go on. Be off with
	    you.
	You disturb my master and you'll catch it.
	Greek aren't you? Well, we don't have no truck
	    with Greeks.

Menelaus	All right, old woman, all right. I understand. But just listen to what I have to say.
Portress	And I say: be off! Go on. I have my orders. Greeks aren't allowed anywhere near here.
Menelaus	Stop that. Get your hands off. Stop pushing me.
Portress	It's your own fault; you won't listen, will you?
Menelaus	Will you just take a message in to your master?
Portress	Not me. It'd be more than my life's worth.
Menelaus	I'm a stranger here – shipwrecked – he wouldn't refuse me.
Portress	Yes, well you go and try that story somewhere else.
Menelaus	I'm coming in, I tell you, so let me past.
Portress	My, but you're a pest. They'll throw you out.
Menelaus	If only I had my soldiers with me now. 520
Portress	You may be a big man with your army, but you're not here.
Menelaus	The indignity of it all! The shame!
Portress	Well, it's no use crying. No one's sorry for you.
Menelaus	I tell you I've known better times...
Portress	Yes, well you go and tell somebody else about it.

71

Menelaus	Just tell me where I am. Whose palace is this?
Portress	This? It's Proteus' palace. You're in Egypt.
Menelaus	Oh no. Not Egypt! How could I possibly . . .
Portress	And what's wrong with Egypt I'd like to know?
Menelaus	Nothing! Nothing! I'm the one who's in the wrong.
Portress	Yes, and you're probably not the only one either.
Menelaus	Your leader – your king, or whatever – is he here?
Portress	Our king's dead. That's his tomb. His son rules now.
Menelaus	Where is *he* then? Indoors? Away somewhere?
Portress	He's not in. Anyway he hates Greeks.
Menelaus	Why? What for? And why should I get the blame?
Portress	It's all because of Helen – Zeus's daughter. She's in there.
Menelaus	What? Who did you say? Say that again.
Portress	Tyndareus' daughter – lived in Sparta.
Menelaus	Where did she come from? What does all this mean? 540
Portress	Come from? She came from Lacedaemon.
Menelaus	When?
	(*aside*) My wife? But I left her in the cave.
	Surely she can't have been carried off again?
Portress	It was before the Greeks had even sailed
	For Troy. But look, it's best if you just go.
	There's been a little bit of bother here.
	You've come at the wrong time. You'd not be welcome.
	If my master found you, he'd likely kill you.
	I've nothing against you Greeks. I know I did speak
	Sharply to you – but, I'm a bit frightened you see.

The Portress goes back into the palace.

Menelaus	I don't understand. What does it all mean?
	This story of hers makes things even worse.
	I go to Troy and recapture my wife.

I bring her here and leave her in a cave.
She's safe there. I know that. Yet now I find
There's some other woman living here,
In this very palace, and with the selfsame name.
And what's more, that old woman said she was
The daughter of Zeus. Can there be a *man*
Called Zeus in Egypt? There's only one Zeus 560
I know of, and he's in heaven. And where on
    earth
Is there another Sparta, except ours,
On the river Eurotas? And Tyndareus.
Now that's a famous name. There can't be two.
And is there another Lacedaemon?
Another Troy? I don't know what to make of
    this.
The world's a big place of course. Lots of men
Must have the same name – cities too – and
    women.
I suppose it's not surprising really.
And the threats of some old servingwoman
Are not going to make me run away.
Besides, no-one could be so barbarous
As to deny me food – well, not once they'd heard
My name. I'm known all over the world.
Menelaus – the man who lit the fires of Troy.
I'll wait here for the master of the house.
There are two courses of action open to me:
If he seems really savage, I'll make a run
For it, and hide somewhere down by the wreck;
But if he shows any sign of friendship   580
I can ask him for the help I need.
It is a bit of a come-down though,
When one king has to go begging to another.
But, that's the way it is. And, as they say,
'There's nothing stronger than necessity.'
Not my own words of course – but true enough
    for all that.

*The Chorus come out of the palace. They do not notice
Menelaus, who anxiously keeps out of their way.*[9]

HELEN

Chorus   We have heard
What the virgin said:
Menelaus is not dead,
Not sunk in the land of gloom
Where dark is the only light.
He is alive;
But wandering wearily over the waves
And kept from his own dear land.
So sick in his heart and lost,
His ship having touched
Every shore save his own
Since he set sail from Troy.

Helen comes from the palace.

Helen   Back then to my post at the tomb, and sanctu-
ary.
I have spoken to Theonoe, and what she said
Was so wonderful. Oh, there is nothing   601
In the world hidden from her. My husband
Is alive! She told me so. He is still alive.
Backwards and forwards, roaming the trackless
sea,
But when his sands of suffering are through
He will come home again. She says so. And yet,
She did not say if he'd come safely home,
And I did not dare to question further.
I was just so glad to know he's still alive.
What's more, she says he's somewhere close at
hand,
Shipwrecked off our coast, and come ashore
With only a few friends left. O Menelaus,
When will I see you? Menelaus, I want you so.

*She sees Menelaus and starts to run for the tomb, but he
is in her way.*

Ah! Who is that? Is this some new scheme
Of Proteus' son to try and trap me?
I must get to the tomb. Bacchantes,
And all wild horses, now grant me your speed.
He looks so wild. And he's coming after me!

HELEN

Menelaus	What are you running for? Wait! What's the matter?
	Why are you trying to get to that altar? 620
	There's nothing to fear! O god, that face.
	What can I say? I don't believe it.
Helen	My women, help me! This man, he won't let me
	Get to the tomb. If they should catch me now
	I'll be married to a man I hate.
Menelaus	I haven't come to hurt you. I'm no criminal.
Helen	But you look as though you are. Those rags![10]
Menelaus	You mustn't be frightened. Don't run away again.
Helen	(*reaching the tomb*)
	No, I won't. Not now I'm here. I'll stay.
Menelaus	Who are you? That face... Lady, tell me who you are.
Helen	Why should I? I don't know who you are.
Menelaus	I never knew two people so alike.
Helen	True knowledge belongs to the gods.
Menelaus	Do you come from these parts? Or are you Greek?
Helen	I am a Greek. A true Hellene. And you?
Menelaus	A true Hellene. You look like Helen to me.
Helen	And you like Menelaus. What can I say?
Menelaus	You're right. Unhappily, I am Menelaus.
Helen	Then I am your wife. Oh, let me hold you.
Menelaus	Wife? You're not... Here, get your hands off my clothes. 640
Helen	The wife Tyndareus, my father, gave you.
Menelaus	O Hecate, send me better dreams than this.
Helen	No goddess sent me. See. I am no dream.
Menelaus	But I can't have two wives either.
Helen	Oh, don't tell me you've got another wife!
Menelaus	I was bringing her back from Troy. She's in a cave.
Helen	Ah! Then you have no other wife at all. Just me.
Menelaus	Am I in my right senses? Am I seeing things?
Helen	Look at me. Don't you recognise your wife?
Menelaus	You do look like her, but I know you can't be.
Helen	Won't you simply look? Now, what other proof do you need?

75

Menelaus	There is a similarity – I don't deny it.
Helen	And your eyes do not deceive you. Trust them.
Menelaus	That's just it. I can't. I have got another wife.
Helen	An image of me only. I never went to Troy.
Menelaus	An image that lives and breathes? How could that be?
Helen	The gods fashioned you a bride out of the very air itself.
Menelaus	The gods. Which gods? Oh, this is beyond me.
Helen	Hera! To thwart Paris. Hera did it.
Menelaus	How could you be at Troy and here at the same time too? 660
Helen	A body's name is free to travel anywhere.
Menelaus	Let me go. I've got troubles enough without this.
Helen	Will you leave me for an empty shadow?
Menelaus	Yes, but since you look like Helen, I wish you well.
Helen	Must I lose you again, just when I've found you?
Menelaus	But all I went through was for her. You can't shake that.
Helen	What am I to do? If he leaves me now, My husband, I'll never see my home again.

Enter the Messenger. He is an old sailor, a member of Menelaus' crew.

Messenger	Menelaus. Oh, I've found you at last, sir. I've been all over this barbaric place Trying to find you. My shipmates sent me.
Menelaus	Did you run into trouble with the natives?
Messenger	Oh, no, sir. Sir, you're not going to believe this.
Menelaus	Well, just tell me. Clearly something's happened, the state you're in.
Messenger	Everything you suffered – it was all for nothing!
Menelaus	I can believe that. But what's happened now?
Messenger	Your wife's gone, sir. Vanished – into thin air. The cave's empty. We had her under guard, But the heavens opened – and up she went – Disappeared. And as she went, she cried out, 680 'You wretched men of Troy, and all you Luckless Greeks who fought, day after day,

HELEN

On the banks of the river Scamander,
Who died in the name of Helen, thinking Paris
Held her there, you were wrong! Wrong! Hera
Deceived you all. Paris never even knew Helen.'
And then she said she'd been here long enough,
Her hour had come, and she was going back –
Back into the sky that had fathered her.
Helen, she said, was innocent,
No matter what the evil tongues of men might
    say.

He notices Helen.

O, my lady! So you've been here all the time!
I was just telling him how you'd gone up –
To the stars. I didn't know you had wings.
Well, you're not going to make fools of us again,
Telling folk we went through all that for nothing.

Menelaus Her story matches his! It must be true!
Oh, let me take you in my arms again.
I've waited so long for this day, Helen.[11]   700

Helen   Menelaus, my dearest,
            How slowly the years without you went,
                And now the joy of you!
                Look, my women, look,
                    A blaze of fire
                    In my darkest night:
                My husband in my arms again!

Menelaus And you in mine. But so much has happened.
There's so much I want to know. Where should I
    begin?

Helen (*tossing her hair*)
                    Even my hair
                    Is alive with joy
            And little tears peep from my eyes
                    To find out why,
                But my arms remember
                What they hold so dear.

Menelaus Indeed there is nothing dearer to me
In all the world than you. Nothing else matters
    now.

77

HELEN

O, Helen, daughter of Zeus and Leda,
Holding you like this brings back that happy day
When your brothers came riding to our wedding.
Do you remember? On their white horses,   720
With torches in their hands; how they cheered.
And then the gods stole you from my house.
But we're together now, and will not part again.
Such good springing from evil; all may now be
   well.

Chorus   And so we pray it will. Where two are one
There is no happiness that is not shared.

Helen   Friends, friends, pains past
        Are pains past grieving for.
          My lord is mine again.
              Mine.
  And the long years at Troy are over.

Menelaus   We have each other now.
They were indeed long years to live through
      Tricked and deceived by the gods.
            If I weep
      My tears have more of joy
        Than grief in them.

Helen   What can I say?
  It is almost more than I had hoped for
    To hold you like this to my heart.   740

Menelaus And you to mine. And all the while we thought
You were in one of those grim towers at Troy.
But Helen, tell me, how were you stolen from my
   house?

Helen   It is a bitter tale you ask for
   And will need bitter words to tell it.

Menelaus Even so. What the gods decree, we must endure.
Helen   I cannot. The words stick in my throat.
Menelaus You must. Troubles overcome have comfort in
   them.

Helen   Not the beat of my heart,
       Nor the beat of their oars
    Carried me off to a bed of lust.

Menelaus What then? What god, what fate was it stole you
   away?

78

HELEN

Helen	It was Hermes, The son of Zeus, Who brought me here to the Nile.
Menelaus	There is something strange and terrible Behind all this. Who sent him?
Helen	I have wept for this And still my eyes are wet with tears. Hera was the cause of all. 760
Menelaus	Hera! What did we ever do to her?
Helen	My torments spring From the very waters Where the goddesses went to bathe When their battle of beauty began.
Menelaus	But why should Hera turn against you?
Helen	To rob Paris of his bride.
Menelaus	But how?
Helen	Aphrodite had promised him *me*!
Menelaus	You!
Helen	So she sent me here to Egypt.
Menelaus	And left him with an image, as you said.
Helen	But – at home – my mother – oh, it's too terrible!
Menelaus	What happened?
Helen	She is dead. Believing me unfaithful to you She hanged herself.
Menelaus	And our daughter – Hermione?
Helen	Safe, but my reputation means No man will ever marry her.
Menelaus	Paris, your deed brought down my house, but you Died too with those ten thousand warriors of Greece. 780
Helen	And I, though innocent, was robbed Of my land, my husband and my name.
Chorus	But the happy days that lie ahead Will atone for all that has passed.
Messenger	Menelaus, sir, I'm not all that sure I understand what's happened. I can tell That it's good news, but I'd like to share it.
Menelaus	I'm sorry, old man, of course you must share it.

79

HELEN

Messenger	Is she not the lady we fought for then?
Menelaus	No, she is not. She never was at Troy.
	They tricked us, the gods, with a kind of phantom.
Messenger	A phantom? Then it was all for nothing? [12]
Menelaus	In a way. We have Hera to thank for that,
	And the quarrel of those three goddesses.
Messenger	This is a real woman though? Your real wife?
Menelaus	She is. You can take my word for that.
Messenger	O my lady, there's no following

The ways of the gods, is there? They're beyond
    us.
It's all topsy-turvy the luck they send us,
Some seem to have bad luck all their lives,   800
Then suddenly – it's over; while others
Are in clover one minute and ruined the next.
You just never know what each new day will
    bring.
You and your husband have had your share
Of troubles. You were sneered and sniggered at.
He was caught up in a war where nothing he did
Made any difference, and yet now
Blessings shower down on him unasked.

So you never did disgrace your father then,
Or your brothers either; it was all lies.

It all comes back to me now – your wedding day:
The horses, four in hand, and me
Running alongside them holding a torch.
And you up there in the chariot
With Menelaus, going off to be married.
Oh, he'd be a poor kind of servant
In my view who didn't live in his master's life,
Sharing his joys, and sharing his sorrows too.
A slave I may be – well, I was born one –
But I hope I am an honourable one   820
With a free man's heart, if not his name.
It'd be a double disaster otherwise:
To be a slave and to feel like one too.

80

HELEN

Menelaus   Old man, you too have borne your share of hard-
          ship,
          In the war at my side, with your shield;
          Now it's time for you to share my triumph.
          Go back to where you left our friends. Tell them
          How you found me here and what has happened.
          But warn them to stay by the shore, to wait there
          Until they see which way this battle goes,
          For a battle there will be, and if I do
          Manage to get my wife away from here
          They must see that no one and nothing
          Stands in the way of our good fortune now.

Messenger   I'll do it, my lord.
                              But there's one thing I must
          say:
          This business of prophecy – it's useless, you
          know,
          Nothing but lies. Burning things on fires,
          Studying birds – sheer lunacy all of it.
          As though birds could do anyone any good.
          Calchas never said anything about this
          When his friends were dying for a phantom.   840
          And no more did Helenus in Troy either
          When his city was under siege for nothing.[13]
          'That's the way the gods wanted it,' you might
          say.
          Then why do we bother with prophets?
          We should forget about them; send up
          Sacrifices to the gods, ask *them* for blessing.
          Prophecy's no more than a bait for greed.
          Nobody ever got rich without hard work.
          I'll tell you what the best kind of prophecy is:
          It's our own common sense, and that's a fact.

          Messenger goes out.

Chorus   The old man is right in what he says.
          A house will have no need of oracles
          While it counts the gods among its friends.

Helen   It's all so wonderful I can't believe it.

81

	But your voyage from Troy, my dear, tell me, was it
	Very awful? It's over now, I know,
	But my love for you makes me want to share it.
Menelaus	Oh, that's a big question; there's so much to tell:
	Ships sunk in the Aegean; men lost; 860
	False lights set up by Nauplius
	On the cliffs at Euboea to try and wreck us;
	Then Crete, and the cities of Libya –
	We were washed up there; Perseus' watch tower.
	Oh, there'd be no end to it. No, no I couldn't;
	I couldn't go through all that again.
Helen	I'm sorry, it was wrong of me to ask.
	Well, never mind, but do tell me one thing:
	How long were you wandering out at sea?
Menelaus	We spent ten years at Troy, then after that –
	Seven – yes, we were seven years at sea.
Helen	Oh, how dreadful! To have lived through all that,
	And to have survived it – only to come here to die.
Menelaus	Die? Here? What are you talking about? [14]
Helen	You must get away as fast as you can.
	If you're found here, you're certain to be killed.
Menelaus	Why? Oh, what have I done to deserve this?
Helen	He wants to marry me, but your coming's stopped that.
Menelaus	Someone was going to marry my wife! Who?
Helen	He's ready to take me by force, I know. 880
Menelaus	How could he? Who is this man? The king?
Helen	Yes, the son of Proteus – he rules here now.
Menelaus	Ah, I see what the old gatekeeper meant.
Helen	Gatekeeper? What gatekeeper? Where else have you been?
Menelaus	Only here. I was almost driven away like a beggar.
Helen	You didn't come begging for food, did you? Surely not?
Menelaus	Well, yes, but I didn't put it quite like that.
Helen	So you know what plans he had for me?

HELEN

Menelaus	Yes. What I don't know is whether you evaded them.
Helen	Menelaus! He never laid a hand on me!
Menelaus	I'd like to believe you. But what proof have I?
Helen	You saw the way I was clinging to that tomb.
Menelaus	Yes, and I see you've got a bed there. What's that for?
Helen	To escape *his* bed. It is sanctuary here.
Menelaus	Don't they have altars? Do they worship tombs here?
Helen	This place is as safe as any temple.
Menelaus	Is there no way we can escape, and get home?
Helen	They'll cut you down before you manage that.
Menelaus	Oh, was ever any man as cursed as I? 903
Helen	You could escape. I wouldn't think it cowardly.
Menelaus	And leave you here? I conquered Troy for your sake.
Helen	I'd rather that than have you die for my sake.
Menelaus	It would be cowardly. I tell you I conquered Troy.
Helen	But I don't think you'll ever kill this king.
Menelaus	Why not? Is he invulnerable to steel?
Helen	You'll see. But I think you'd be silly to try.
Menelaus	I'll just quietly let him take me, shall I?
Helen	It won't be easy. We'd need to be very cunning.
Menelaus	If I'm going to die, I'll die fighting.
Helen	As I see it, there's only one way.
Menelaus	What is it? Bribery, force, or persuasion?
Helen	If we can somehow stop him knowing that you're here.
Menelaus	Who'll tell him? He won't recognise me like this.
Helen	In there he has an ally, wise as any god.
Menelaus	Some sort of divine voice in the walls, do you mean?
Helen	No. His sister. She's called Theonoe.
Menelaus	That's an ominous name. Tell me about her.
Helen	She knows everything. She'll tell him you are here.
Menelaus	Well, that's that then. There's nowhere I can hide.

83

Helen	But if we could win her onto our side.	920
Menelaus	What do you mean? What do you think she could do?	
Helen	If she'd agree not to tell her brother.	
Menelaus	Yes, if she agrees to that, we're safe.	
Helen	Yes, if. But without her help, we have no hope.	
Menelaus	You'd better do it. She'll listen to a woman.	
Helen	I'll throw myself at her feet.	
Menelaus	Yes, but what if she won't listen, what then?	
Helen	Then you'll be dead, and I forced to marry.	
Menelaus	Forced? That's just a word. An excuse. I don't like this.	
Helen	I swear on my oath – I swear on my life –	
Menelaus	You'll die rather than give yourself to him?	
Helen	By the sword that kills you, I swear I will die too.	
Menelaus	Take my hand. That's a promise we will seal.	
Helen	I solemnly swear that if you die, I die too.	
Menelaus	And if I lose you, I'll end my life. I swear it.	
Helen	And we will do it with honour. How shall we do it?	
Menelaus	I'll kill you here by the tomb. Then I'll kill myself.	

Menelaus (cont.)
But I'll put up a struggle for you first,
I tell you. Let 'em all come. I don't care.   939
I'll not smirch the honour that I won at Troy.
I'm not going back to Greece and have them say
That I, who brought about the death of Thetis'
   son,
Achilles – who saw Ajax fall on his sword –
Who left Nestor childless – that I, Menelaus,
Was not man enough to die for his own wife!
Never! If the great gods of war are wise,
When a man dies with honour at the hands
Of his foes, the earth lies light upon his grave.
Cowards are flung to rot among the rocks!

Chorus   May the gods at last
Bless the House of Tantalus
And keep you from all harm.

Voices are heard inside the palace.

Helen   Oh, no! The Fates are not through with me yet!

HELEN

It's too late, Menelaus. We're finished!
Theonoe's coming. I can hear them
Unbolting the doors. We've nowhere to run.
She'll know that you're here whether she sees
    you or not.
It is all over. You escaped from Troy
Only to die on these savages' swords.

*Enter Theonoe preceded by a procession of attendants
bearing torches and incense.*

Theonoe   Lead on with your torches and let the rites begin.
Burn and purge the air. Now the incense. Come.
Only the purest breath of heaven must we
    breathe.   962
And if unhallowed feet have fouled the way
Cleanse it with your holy fire that I may pass.
And when the ceremony's done, let the flame
Be borne with reverence into the temple.

Well, Helen, did I not tell you? Your lord,
Menelaus, is come. And there he stands.
His ships all lost and gone. And gone too
The image of you that he had. Poor man!
So many dangers overcome, and yet
Still not knowing if he'll ever reach his home.
And if you linger here, you never will.
For in the courts of heaven today, the gods
Meet in high council to decide your case.
And Hera, once your foe, but now your friend,
Will plead for both of you to be allowed
Safe passage home. She wants the Greeks to
    know
The truth of Aphrodite's trickery.
But Aphrodite will thwart you if she can,   980
Do anything so no-one ever learns
She won her prize for beauty by a cheat.
But the issue rests with me. I could do
What Aphrodite wants, and tell my brother
You are here. Or, I could side with Hera,
Decide to save your life, and say nothing,

85

Though his orders were to tell him instantly.

Go someone, tell my brother he is here;
The safety of my own position must come first.

Helen Theonoe, no! Look, I kneel to you,
In abject supplication at your feet.
Have pity on us. Have I found him
After all these years only to see him die?
Now that I hold him in my arms again
Do not betray him to your brother.
Spare us, I beseech you. Don't sacrifice
Your own good name for reverence and right
And buy your brother's thanks with such a
    wrong.
The gods, we know, abhor all violence.
They tell us to possess what's ours by right
Not might. What's won by evil is unclean.   1000
The sky and earth are common to us all,
And their fruits belong to all, but no man
May wrest by force what is by right another's.
When I first came here, it was a blessing,
Or so it seemed. Hermes had given me
To your father, as his ward, to keep me safe
For my husband, Menelaus, and now
He is here. He has come back to claim me.
But how can he if you kill him? How can
Your father give the living to the dead?
And your father gave his word, remember,
Pledged it to the gods. Their integrity
Is the issue here. Would they or would they not
Want what is rightfully another's
To be given back? I think they would.
The whims of your wild brother must not be
    raised
Above the mandate of your noble father.
Can a prophetess, one who sees and knows
The ways of god, prevent the wishes   1020
Of a righteous man, to gorge a brother's lust?
I would be ashamed to have your knowledge,
To know what is and was and ever shall be,

86

HELEN

Yet not know wrong from right. Have pity.
Misfortune and misery surround us,
But we are together and you can save us.
The name of Helen is reviled throughout the
    world.
All Hellas claims that I forsook my lord
For the pampered luxury of Troy,
But if I can go back to Greece, go back
To Sparta, and let the people hear and see
That it was the malice of the gods
That ruined them, not I; if I can prove
I never was untrue, my reputation
May be saved, and my poor daughter, whom all
    men shun,
May yet find marriage, happiness and love.
Oh, put an end to my dreary exile.
Let me live again in my own home.
If Menelaus had died in those wars
I should have wept for him from afar.   1040
But he is here, and alive. You cannot take him
    now.

Theonoe, I beg you, grant me your grace.
Let your heart be noble, and let people say
That you followed the ways of your father.

Chorus   O Helen, to see you and to hear you
Is to pity you. But what, I wonder,[15]
Will Menelaus say to save his life?

Menelaus   Well, I'm not going to throw myself at your feet
And start weeping, so don't expect it.
Why, the very ghosts of Troy would blush if I
    did that.
Mind you, I've heard it said that weeping does
    sometimes
Befit a hero, when things are going wrong.
All the same though, that's not my way. My way is
Courage.
          So, if you are going to help us,
And, as I feel you are duty bound,
To give me back my wife, then do so. If not,

87

HELEN

Well, it won't be my first taste of misery,
But it would be very wicked of you.
And now, if you please, my plea for justice,
Which is no more, I think, than I deserve,   1060
I will make – and this ought to touch your heart –
With due reverence, to your father's grave.

Most reverend sir, at whose tomb I stand,
I ask you for the return of my wife
Whom Zeus himself put into your safekeeping.
You're dead, I know, and can't do it yourself,
But surely she will never let her father's name –
That glorious name I now invoke –
Be sullied in this way. It's up to her.

And now to the gods of the underworld.
I call on your help too. Many men
I've sent to you on account of Helen,
Men that I killed. Oh, yes, I've paid my dues.
Well now I want them back alive again;
Yes, either that, or you make this woman
Show herself more noble than her father,
And give me back my wife.

(*to Theonoe*)   Because, if you don't,
I'll tell you something she forgot to mention,
And you'd better listen. I've sworn on oath
To take on your brother single-handed.   1080
Either he kills me or I kill him. And that's that.
And if he's not got the courage – if he tries
To besiege us here in our sanctuary
And starve us out, then you know what I'll do?
I'll kill her first, then plunge this two-edged
    sword
Right through my own heart – yes, here on the
    tomb,
So that our blood runs down your father's grave.
And here we'll lie, side by side, on this stone
A mortal insult to your father's name.
Your brother won't marry her. Nobody will.

88

HELEN

Either I take her home – or to the grave!　　1260
Yes, I'm threatening you! And do you know
　why?
Because tears may win pity, but never battles.
You can kill me now, but your shame will live
　on.
Better to do what I say:
Do what is right and give me back my wife.

Chorus It is time to judge. You have heard them both.
May your judgement be pleasing to all.

Theonoe I am, both by my nature and my will,
Moved towards charity; zealous too　　1100
For the safety of my soul, and my father's name.
I cannot lead my brother into sin.
My heart is a temple of justice
Founded by my father's father, Nereus.
Therefore, Menelaus. I shall try,
Since it is Hera's will, to save you;
And may Aphrodite, Queen of Love,
Forgive me – although such love has been
No part of my life, nor ever shall.
Those taunts you made over my father's grave
I must, of course, accept. Were he alive,
He would give back your wife, and so must I.
For what we do on earth, we are rewarded,
And so it is beyond. Life as we know it
There may not be, when the souls of the dead
Are with the immortal spirit blended,
But immortal understanding still survives.

In short, I shall, as you ask, keep silent
And do nothing to assist my brother's lust;
Thereby, perhaps, rendering him more service
Than his heart as yet can comprehend.　　1121

But that is all I'll do. How you escape
Is up to you. Pray now to the gods;
Ask Aphrodite for safe passage home,
And pray that Hera, who is now your friend,
May never change her mind.
　　　　　　　　Father, this I swear,

89

HELEN

No deeds of mine shall ever disgrace your name.

Theonoe goes back into the palace.

Chorus	See, the ways of sinners never prosper.
	Good earns its own reward.
Helen	So, Menelaus, we've nothing to fear
	From her. Can we do it, do you think?
	Can we work out some plan of escape?
Menelaus	Listen, tell me: you've been here a long time,
	Are you on friendly terms with the servants?
Helen	Yes, I believe so. But why do you ask?
	Have you thought of a way to save us?
Menelaus	Could someone in the stables be persuaded
	To let us have a chariot and horses?
Helen	They could be, perhaps. But no, that's no use.
	We don't know the roads; we'd be sure to be caught. 1140
Menelaus	I suppose you're right. I could hide in the palace
	And kill him. I've got my sword. What about that?
Helen	No, his sister would never allow that.
	She'd warn him if she thought you meant to kill him.
Menelaus	Well, what then? We haven't got a ship.
	Ours is at the bottom of the sea.
Helen	I know I'm only a woman, but...
	Would you let me tell them that you're dead?[16]
Menelaus	I don't much like the sound of that, but yes,
	If you think it'll do any good.
Helen	Of course it would. I could go to the king
	Weeping and wailing, with my hair shorn, and...
Menelaus	No, it all sounds a bit silly to me.
	Anyway, I don't see where it would get us.
Helen	I'll tell him you were drowned at sea
	Then I can ask him for a coffin for you.
Menelaus	Even if he agreed, what use would that be?
	A coffin's not going to help me escape.
Helen	It will if I ask him for a ship 1160
	So I can bury you at sea.

90

HELEN

Menelaus	That's a really good idea. Wait though, / What if he tells you to bury me here?
Helen	I'll tell him it's against all our customs: / If you die at sea, you can't be buried on shore.
Menelaus	That ought to do it, I think. And of course / I would be on board the ship with you.
Helen	Yes, of course. Of course you'll be on the ship / With all the others who escaped the wreck.
Menelaus	Just let me and my crew get on that ship / And man for man we'll hold it with our swords.
Helen	Yes, well that's something I must leave to you. / All we need is good speed and a fair wind.
Menelaus	And we'll have it. The gods will help us now. / But who are you going to say told you of my death?
Helen	You. We'll tell him you're the sole survivor / Of Menelaus' crew; you saw him die.
Menelaus	That's good. He'll never recognise me, / And these rags will support my shipwreck story.
Helen	Yes, oddly enough, they're a stroke of luck; / The state you're in will be the saving of us. 1180
Menelaus	Do you think I should come in there with you? / Or shall I just sit here by the tomb?
Helen	You stay here. If he should get violent / Then you'll have the sanctuary of the tomb / As well as your sword to rely on. / I'll go inside, cut my hair, scratch my face / And change this white robe for a black one. / It's a risk, I know, but it has to be taken. / And there are only two ways it can go: / If he sees through our plot, we'll both be dead, / If he doesn't then we're home and safe.

O Hera, Queen of Heaven,
To your star-wrought home we lift our hands
In humble supplication
And beseech you to grant us your aid.

And Dione's daughter, Aphrodite,
Through me you won the prize for beauty,
Do not destroy me now. It seemed like death

91

HELEN

When you ruined my good name, but I pray you,
Let me die in my own land. Oh, why is it   1200
The Queen of Love should thirst for evil so?
Why work your will through intrigues, lies and
  lust,
evil Passions and potions that send men to their
  death?
No gift of the gods surpasses love
love good When it comes in peace and with tenderness.

Helen goes into the palace.

Chorus   Nightingale,[17]
                          lend me your voice;
                      Shy bird
                          brown bird,
                      Whose sad notes
                          ripple the dark, green
                      Veil of the forest.

                          Come to me
                      Little queen bird
                          little
                      Brown bird,
                          lend me your voice
                      And share with me
                          my new song's
                              sorrow.   1220

A song that will tell of Helen's grief,
And the Trojan women's tears
When they stooped beneath the yoke
Of the Grecian army's spears.

A doom that dates from the day that Paris
Sped over the seas from Sparta
Thinking Helen was his bride.

Greeks died too:
Gored through with spears,
Heads smashed with stones.
Down into the dark of Hades
So many sad souls marched,

92

HELEN

While widows wept in lonely rooms
And tore at their hair in their grief.

One false flare
Lit by one solitary sailor
Wrecked a whole fleet:
Towards it they sailed –
Like a star it lured them –
And their keels ripped on the rocks;   1240
Thousands sank to their deaths.

But wild waters
Seized Menelaus
And flung him about on the sea
With only that mockery Helen –
That phantom for his prize.

Search as you will
To the ends of the earth
To the end of time,
Would you hope
To find out god –
Or even
What is not god –
When you see how his words
Send you this way
And that way,
Even spinning you back
To the void?

No, nothing is ever certain.
Helen had Zeus for a father –   1260
Could there be a greater glory?
Like a swan he swooped
And left his seed
In the womb of Leda, her mother.
But she lived to be cursed
By the people of Greece even so:
'Adulteress' they called her.
'Adulteress – treacherous and godless!'
No, nothing is ever certain
That comes from the mouth of man,

HELEN

Only the word of god,
So I have found, is true.

war → It is madness to put your faith
In the strength of the spear in your hand,
In the biting edge of a sword;
Trusting in war to bring you fame,
Trusting in war to bring you peace.
XX War brings nothing but wounds and grief.
War strikes dumb the voice of reason.
War set fire to the walls of Troy.   1280
War brought death to the sons of Troy.
Slavery, misery, blood and hate,
And the all-engulfing dark of death –
These are the gifts of war.

*Enter Theoclymenus with his attendants leading hounds
and carrying hunting gear.*

Theoclymenus   Wait. Stay where you are until I've paid my
respects
To my father's tomb, built here by these gates
So that each day as we go out and in
Our eyes may see it and remember him.
Proteus, I, Theoclymenus, your son,
Do greet and honour you.

Right, take the dogs
inside
And see those nets are put away carefully.

The attendants go inside.

I think I'm getting too soft with that lot.
One or two put to death would wake their ideas
up.
I've just been told some Greek has landed here,
Quite openly, and got past my guards.
Looking for some way to rescue Helen no doubt.
But he'll be caught, and once he is, he's dead.

He suddenly turns back to the tomb.

94

Good god! I'm too late. They've done it!
There's nobody there. They must have taken
  her.
You there! Open those doors! Get the horses out!
And the chariots! Come on! Look to it!   1301
They're not going to get away with this.
Not if I can help it. That woman's mine!

The doors are opened and he sees Helen.

No. Wait. It's all right. She hasn't gone.
She's in the palace. I can see her.

Enter Helen in black and with her hair shorn.

Why, Helen. What's this? Why are you all in
  black?
You've cut your hair. And your cheeks are wet.
You've been crying. What's the matter?
Has something upset you? Bad dreams?

Helen	My lord – and now indeed you are my lord – My hopes are dashed. My life is finished.
Theoclymenus	Why? What is it? Tell me what's happened.
Helen	Menelaus – oh, I can't say it – he's dead.
Theoclymenus	Dead? Oh, I'm sorry – well I'm sorry for you, But to me this is wonderful news. But how did you hear? Did someone tell you?
Helen	Yes, someone who was with him when he died.
Theoclymenus	Someone who was there? It must be true then.
Helen	Yes, and he's here. But I would he were not.
Theoclymenus	Who is he? Where is he? I want to get this straight. 1320
Helen	Over there, cowering behind the tomb.
Theoclymenus	Good god! What a state he's in. He's in rags.
Helen	And to think that my husband may have looked like this.
Theoclymenus	But who is he, and where has he come from?
Helen	He's a Greek. He sailed with my husband.
Theoclymenus	Did he tell you how Menelaus died?
Helen	Most pitifully. He was drowned.
Theoclymenus	Yes, but where? Where was he sailing to?
Helen	His ship went down off the coast of Libya.
Theoclymenus	If he was on the same ship, how was *he* saved?

95

HELEN

Helen	Common people sometimes have uncommon luck.
Theoclymenus	But how is it he's here? Where's the ship now?
Helen	Oh, if only he were sunk too, and not my Menelaus.
Theoclymenus	Menelaus *is* drowned though. But how did he get here?
Helen	Some sailors found him and took him on board, he says.
Theoclymenus	And that phantom that took your place in Troy?
Helen	It vanished into thin air.
Theoclymenus	Then Troy and Priam perished for nothing.
Helen	And not alone. Their fate is mine also.
Theoclymenus	Did they manage to bury your husband's body, or... 1340
Helen	No, that's the worst of it. He's still unburied.
Theoclymenus	That's why you cut your hair, I suppose.
Helen	My husband still means everything to me.
Theoclymenus	It is the truth you're telling me, isn't it?
Helen	Could I in any way deceive your sister?
Theoclymenus	No, that's true. Well, will you leave this tomb now?
Helen	Oh, grant me some little while for grief.
Theoclymenus	But you can't go on avoiding me.
Helen	No, that's all over now. You may make the arrangements.
Theoclymenus	I've waited so long to hear those words.
Helen	You know what must be done. Let us forget the past.
Theoclymenus	Oh, you've made me so happy. What can I do in return?
Helen	Simply forgive me. Let there be peace between us.
Theoclymenus	With all my heart. Look, all my anger's gone.
Helen	And on my knees, I ask you, as a friend...
Theoclymenus	Anything. Anything. There's no need to beg.
Helen	My dead husband – I would like to bury him.
Theoclymenus	Bury him? How? You can't bury a ghost.
Helen	It's our custom for those who die at sea.

96

Theoclymenus	Is it? What is? I'm not familiar with your customs. 1360
Helen	We take an empty shroud with all due rites ...
Theoclymenus	Yes, of course. I'll build a tomb. Anywhere you like.
Helen	No. No. Not a tomb. That's not our way.
Theoclymenus	What then? I said I didn't understand.
Helen	We take our offerings out onto the sea.
Theoclymenus	Ah. Now, what kind of things would you like?
Helen	(*pointing to Menelaus*)
	He can tell you. I've no experience of this.
Theoclymenus	Well, friend, this is good news you've brought us.
Menelaus	Not for me. Nor is it for the dead.
Theoclymenus	Tell me,
	How do you bury people who've been drowned at sea?
Menelaus	With what ceremony his rank calls for.
Theoclymenus	Oh, never mind the cost. For her I'll do anything.
Menelaus	An offering of blood first to the underworld.
Theoclymenus	Any animal you like – just name it.
Menelaus	It's up to you. Whatever you think would be best.
Theoclymenus	With us it's usually a bull, or a horse.
Menelaus	Yes, well, so long as it's in good condition.
Theoclymenus	Oh, never fear. We have some very fine beasts here.
Menelaus	Then a bier and robes – even though there's no body.
Theoclymenus	Yes, we can do that. And anything else? 1380
Menelaus	Some bronze armour. Menelaus always liked spears.
Theoclymenus	I'll find one worthy of him.
Menelaus	And food too. Fruit. Something like that.
Theoclymenus	What? And you'll throw all this in the sea?
Menelaus	Yes. So we'll need a ship, and oarsmen too.
Theoclymenus	How far out will you need to take it?
Menelaus	Oh, some way out beyond the breakers.
Theoclymenus	Why so far? What's the point of that?
Menelaus	So the tide doesn't wash it all back in again.

97

Theoclymenus	Ah. I've got a fine Phoenician vessel – really fast.
Menelaus	That'll be very good. Menelaus would like that.
Theoclymenus	You can do all this yourself, can't you. You don't need Helen?
Menelaus	A man's mother, wife or child must be there.
Theoclymenus	I see. That's how it has to be, is it?
Menelaus	Piety demands it. The dead must be given their due.

Theoclymenus Then she will go. As my wife, she must
Be dutiful. Go into the palace
And take whatever you need.

          And you,
I assure you, will not leave empty-handed.
Kindness such as yours must be rewarded.
That was good news you brought me –
In return I'll find you some new clothes   1400
So you can get out of those rags – food too.
And I'll make sure you get home again to
   Greece.

And Helen – no more tears now – Menelaus
Is dead, and there's nothing can bring him back.

Menelaus Well, lady, you know where your duty lies.
Here stands your husband; you must accept
  him.
The other is nothing to you now.
All will be for the best – you'll see.
And when I get back to Greece, I'll put a stop
To the tales they've been telling about you –
If you can show yourself a true wife now.

Helen I will, and, as you are my witness,
My husband shall have not the slightest cause
To complain of me.
          Go in now.
You must be tired. Take a bath and change your
  clothes.
I'll see you are rewarded right away.
For if you have from me what you deserve,
You will, I think, be all the readier   1442
To do those duties proper to my lord.[18]

98

HELEN

Helen, Theoclymenus and Menelaus all go into the palace.

Chorus   You have heard the tale [19]
Of the great goddess-mother, Demeter:
How she lost her daughter
And went running through the forest,
Running down the mountain,
Out-leaping in her frenzy
Even rivers in full spate;
Seeking and searching;
Searching through the thunderous
Surge of the sea;
Searching for a daughter
Men dare not name;
Though *her* voice called her,
'Persephone! Persephone!'
Again and again
With a sound like echoing cymbals.
The lions of Cybele she yoked
To a mighty chariot of war
And with her   1440
Artemis went
The storm-footed virgin
Goddess of the Bow,
And grey-eyed Pallas
With her battle shield and spear;
And together they rode
In quest of the child
Old Hades stole
As she danced
With her friends in a ring.

But Zeus
On his throne in heaven
Had other plans in mind.

When all her wanderings were over,
Her weary searching all in vain,
She climbed the snow-bound slopes of Mount
   Ida

HELEN

And sank to the ground in her grief.

Grief that reached out
And grasped the land,
That shrivelled the grass
And parched the fields.   1460
Flesh was pinched to the bone –
Men starved –
Cattle staggered and fell.

The cities went silent.
In their temples
All the fires on the altars
Went out,
For there was nothing left
To sacrifice.

But when the altars on earth are cold,
The feasts of the gods fail too,
And Zeus, to soothe her wrath,
Sent for the Graces, and said,
'Go now, go down
And find this sorrowing mother,
Such pain must be assuaged.
With dancing and with singing –
The Muses will show you how –
You must lift this cloud from her heart.'   1480

And with them went Aphrodite,
Fairest of the immortals,
Running to the rhythm of the tabor,
Her voice
Singing over the cymbals.

And Demeter smiled
And raised to her lips
A silver flute
Whose sweet sound
Cured all care.

O princess,

HELEN

Did you neglect her rites?
Were they only the false
Fires of love
That you kindled in your rooms?
Was that what raised
Her anger?

Oh, beware of the anger of the gods,
When the Bacchae come dancing   1500
In their dappled-white fawnskins
Holding their thyrsi high in the air,
With their wild hair streaming
In the light of the moon
And you hear the voice of their drums,

Beware the power of the gods:,
Your only power
Was your beauty.

*warning to
Helen*

Enter Helen.

Helen   O, my friends, it's all going so well.
Theoclymenus questioned her
But she kept her word; she didn't tell him
Menelaus was here. She said he was dead.
And do you know what Menelaus did?
He said he would need armour and weapons
To cast into the sea as part of the rites.
And now he's put that armour on –
A shield in his left hand, a spear in his right,
Ready to cut down those Egyptian troops
As soon as we are safely on the ship.
Oh, you should see him now.   1520
He's got rid of those rags, and had a bath;
I've given him new clothes, and . . .
                                          But sh!
It's Theoclymenus, and he still thinks
I'm going to marry him. Say nothing please.
And when we can, we will come back for you.

*Enter Menelaus, armed, and Theoclymenus with atten-
dants who are carrying offerings for the funeral.*

101

Theoclymenus	You men, take those things down to the harbour,
	And do exactly what this man tells you.
	Helen, I'd rather – that is, if you don't mind –
	Well, I'd rather it if you stayed here.
	I mean – well, you'll have done your duty by him
	Whether you go or not, and I'm worried
	Lest it all prove too upsetting for you,
	And – in your grief – you throw yourself in the sea.
	Anyway, don't you think perhaps you're taking this
	Too far. After all, there's no body, and ...
Helen	O, my dearest – husband – may I call you that?
	Custom demands that I honour him
	Who took me as his bride. Yes, I loved him,
	And if my death could help him, I would gladly die,
	But as I know it will not, let me go 1540
	And do what's right, and after that
	Then may the gods grant all my wishes
	For you, and for this stranger who has helped us so.
	And for your kindness to me, and to my lord
	I will be all the wife that you deserve.
	The future, I feel, holds so much for us.
	Now, for my sake, to show your love for me –
	We need a ship. Won't you give the order?
Theoclymenus	Of course. You – one of the Sidonian vessels,
	A fifty-oar. Make sure it has a full crew.
Helen	This man will be in charge of the crew, won't he?
Theoclymenus	Yes, yes. My men will do what he says.
Helen	Could you tell them again, so they really do?
Theoclymenus	Again and again, yes, if that's what you want.
Helen	My blessings on you – on us both indeed.
Theoclymenus	Now, now, that's enough. No more tears.
Helen	Very soon you'll see just how grateful I am.
Theoclymenus	But the dead are nothing; this is such a waste.
Helen	I must remember the dead and the living.
Theoclymenus	I'll be a good husband – good as Menelaus. 1560
Helen	That's all I ask. Just give me time.

102

HELEN

Theoclymenus	I'll give you all you ask – if you'll give me your heart.
Helen	Believe me, my heart knows where it belongs.
Theoclymenus	My dearest – shall I come with you?
Helen	No. No, such things are for servants, not kings.
Theoclymenus	You're right. And no doubt best left to you Greeks.

You understand them. He did not die here,
So my house is in no way tainted by it.

Go, one of you, and tell my loyal subjects
They may bring their presents to the palace now.
Let the whole land sing out with hymns of joy
To celebrate this happy wedding day.

(*to Menelaus*)
You, stranger, away with you now. Take these gifts
And cast them upon the waters of the sea
To honour him who was her husband once.
When that's done, bring her back, quick as you can
And you may join our table at the wedding feast.
You're welcome to stay on after too, if you like.

Theoclymenus and his attendants go out.

Menelaus	(*praying*)

O wisest and most reverend Zeus,
Look smilingly upon our plans,   1580
And as we struggle up high Fortune's hill,
Stretch out your hand –
One little touch –
A finger tip –
And we are home.
We have suffered much,
Enough I think. But never
Have I neglected
What is due to you.

103

HELEN

Our miseries should know some end.
Grant me this prayer.
Grant our life joy.

Helen and Menelaus go off together.

Chorus Yes grant, oh grant [20]
That this vessel from Sidon
Be cradled in foam
On a tranquil sea;
Speed her home safely
Attended by dolphins
That plunge through the waves at her prow.
Oh harden the arms   1600
Of the oarsmen who pull her
Safely home to the shores of Greece,
Oh, shake out their sails for them,
Queen of the calm,
And fill them with winds
That will sing to the sailors
Urging them home to safe harbour in Greece.

Greece:
Where Helen may see
The daughters of Leucippus
Down by the river Eurotas;
Or when midsummer comes,
At the temple of Pallas,
The people of Sparta
Who dance for the death
Of poor Hyacinthus
Slain by the discus of Apollo. [21]
And on that day
When feasts are held
And offerings made   1620
As the son of Zeus ordained,
She may see among the dancers
Her daughter Hermione,
A virgin whom still
No man will wed.

HELEN

Oh, if only we
Had wings
And could fly with the cranes
When winter comes
And they leave behind
The cold and the rain.
Up in the air they go
Following their leader
Down into Libya
Where the land is dry
And yellow with wheat.

Oh, fly!
Stretch out your long necks and fly!
Higher than the clouds
Fly   1640
Up to the Pleiades,
Outstrip Orion
As he strides through the night.
Fly on, oh fly
And trumpet out the news
That Troy's destroyer
Menelaus himself
Is heading for home!

You brothers of Helen,
Whose home is in heaven,
Ride!
Spur your great stallions
Down the storms of the air!
Be near her.
Guard her.
When the waters turn white
And the sky goes dark
Then trample down
Those horses of the sea!
Calm she needs and peace.   1660
Peace, and an end to those tales that tell
Of her lust in a foreign bed.

Must she suffer for ever

HELEN

Because goddesses quarrel?
Trample down such slander!
Tell them!
Helen never went to Troy!

*Enter Theoclymenus from the palace and a Messenger
from the harbour.*

Messenger   Your majesty, I'm sorry,
But I bring the most terrible news.

Theoclymenus   What is it?

Messenger   You'll need to find
Another bride. Helen's gone.

Theoclymenus   Gone? What do you mean? Has she flown?

Messenger   Yes, with Menelaus. That man who brought the news
Of his death was Menelaus himself.

Theoclymenus   I don't believe it. How did it happen?

Messenger   Didn't you yourself give him a ship?

Theoclymenus   Yes, but how? How could he overpower
The whole crew? That's what I want to know.
Weren't you one of them?

Messenger   Yes. Let me explain.[22] 1680
We left the palace, and went down to the harbour
With Helen, the daughter of Zeus,
Cunningly bewailing the death of her husband
Every step of the way, though of course
He was there beside her all the time.
When we got there, we chose the swiftest vessel
We could find, a Sidonian with fifty oars
Just as you said.
            Well, we got it launched,
And every man took up his post:
Some stepped the mast, others ran out the oars;
The white sails were folded and set;
The rudder fixed in position and lashed.

And while all this was going on, some men
Came down to the shore; they must have been watching

106

And waiting for just the right moment.
Greeks they were, Menelaus' old crew.
They were all in rags, and filthy,
But they had a certain something about them
For all that. When Menelaus saw them
He put on a fine show of pity and said,   1700
'Oh, what happened to you? Whose ship were
   you on?'
And then, 'Seeing you're Greeks, won't you
   come and help us
Honour the fallen son of Atreus?
His wife, the lady Helen here,
Is going to perform the ceremony.'
Then they wept – oh, it was all done so well –
And started to help us load the offerings.
There did seem to be rather a lot of them
And some of us began to get a bit
Suspicious, but we didn't say anything.
Well, I mean, we'd had our orders, hadn't we?
You gave him complete command, didn't you?
That was the trouble.
                   Anyway, most of the stuff
We had to load was light enough,
And everything was going smoothly
Until we came to that bull. It would not budge.
No way could we get it onto the gangplank.
It just stood there, rolling its eyes and bellowing,
Lowering its horns, and tossing its head.
None of us could get anywhere near it.   1720
Then Helen's husband called out, 'You men,
You men who laid waste Troy, come on now,
Let's do it the Greek way; get that beast
Up on your shoulders and heave it over the side.'
Then he waved his sword and shouted again
And they did it. They just picked it up
And threw it onto the ship.
                 There was a horse too,
But Menelaus simply patted its neck
And it followed him on board.
                 And that was that.

HELEN

Everything was ready, Helen came up on deck
And calmly sat herself down next to her 'dead'
   husband,
While the other Greeks positioned themselves
In various parts of the ship; each one
As we were to find out later, with a sword
Hidden under his rags.
                But the bosun
Gave us the order to row, and our song
Rang out as our oars cut deep into the waves.
It wasn't long before we were almost
Out of sight of the land, and the helmsman said,
'Is this far enough, friend, or do you want us
To go out further? It's up to you.'   1741
'No, this will do', said Menelaus,
And took his sword and went up to the prow
To slay the bull; but as he cut its throat,
There was no dead man's name on his lips. No,
'Poseidon', he prayed, 'and all you chaste
Nereids of the sea, take us home!
Yes, me and Helen, my wife, take us home!'
And the bull's blood spurted out into the water
As he spoke. That was a bad omen for us.
'Treachery!' shouted one of my mates. 'Quick!
We've got to get back. Ship your oars, left bank!
Pull on the right, and get your helm over!'
But towering over the dead bull,
Menelaus shouted to his men,
'Right, lads! Now! For Greece! Jump to it!
Cut 'em down and throw 'em overboard!'
And our bosun was yelling, 'Defend yourselves!
Use your oars, break that bench up, anything!
Use anything – just smash their heads in!'   1760
We did what we could, but it was wood against
   swords;
The ship ran with blood. And there was Helen,
Up in the stern, cheering them on:
'Now then, show these peasants how you fought
   at Troy!'
And we fought too; some fell, and struggled up

108

To their feet, then fell again and were dead.
But Menelaus was in armour, remember,
And wherever he saw his men in trouble
He was there with his sword. Some of our men
Flung themselves overboard in their terror.
Those who stayed are all dead – except, that is
The helmsman, and they made him set course
    for Greece.
They hoisted sail, and even the wind was right.
And so they've gone.
            I only got away
By climbing down the anchor chain. And I
    almost drowned.
But some fishermen found me and brought me
    ashore
So that I could bring you this message.

We were taken in. Let's never forget that,
And never trust too soon again.

Messenger goes out.

Chorus	My lord, I would never have believed 1779
	Menelaus could be here and we not know it.
Theoclymenus	Wouldn't you? Women! They're liars, all of
	them!

She said she was going to marry me!
Oh, if there was only some way I could catch
That ship...
         But never mind. Theonoe's still here.
I'll be revenged on her, traitor that she is.
She saw Menelaus, and said nothing.
But she'll never do it again. I'll see to that!

*He draws his sword and starts to rush into the palace,
but one of Theonoe's servants comes out and bars his
way.*

Servant	My lord, think what you're doing. You can't
	murder her!
Theoclymenus	This isn't murder, it's justice. Get out of my way!
Servant	No, I won't let you do it.

109

Theoclymenus	Have a care, slave.
Servant	It's for your own good.
Theoclymenus	Let me past.
Servant	No.
Theoclymenus	She has got to die.
Servant	What she did was right.
Theoclymenus	Right? She betrayed me!
Servant	For your honour's sake.
Theoclymenus	Giving my wife to another man!
Servant	But she was his.
Theoclymenus	She was mine!
Servant	Her father gave her to him.
Theoclymenus	But Fortune gave her to me.
Servant	And Fate took her away again.
Theoclymenus	You can't judge me.
Servant	In this I think I can.
Theoclymenus	Who's king?
Servant	Who's right?
Theoclymenus	You know that you're asking to die.
Servant	All right. Kill me. If you can. But you won't
	Kill your sister, not while I'm alive. 1800
	I am her servant and will gladly give my life for her.

The Dioscuri, Helen's twin brothers, appear in the air.

Dioscuri	King of Egypt, stop![23]
	Theoclymenus, you must stop this madness!

We are the Dioscuri – the sons of Zeus
And Leda, brothers of that same Helen
Who has fled your house.
                          You are angry.
You are angry that you have lost your bride.
But she was never meant to be a bride for you.
Your sister, Theonoe, has done no wrong.
She followed the will of heaven
And obeyed your father's commands.
For it was so ordained that Helen

110

HELEN

Should dwell within these walls
Until such time as Troy was burned
In her borrowed name.
Now that is done she must return
To her proper husband,
And her own true home.

Put up your murderous sword.
A more than mortal wisdom
Has your sister shown.
We two, raised to divinity,
Thought long ago to rescue Helen,
But even as gods
Our power was as nothing
Against the will of heaven.

So much, Theoclymenus, for you.
Now, hear us, Helen.
Sail on with your husband
And may fair winds go with you.
We two will ride the salt sea's waves
And guard you to your home,
And when your term of mortal life is done,
You will, with us, become divine,
With us be worshipped
And revered on earth,
For such too is the will of heaven.

And that same island
Where Hermes paused
On his way from Sparta
Whence he had stolen you
To keep you safe from Paris,
Men will henceforward know as Helena.

And for Menelaus,
Who has wandered so,
Heaven has decreed a home
On the Island of the Blest.
Such noble hearts as his
The gods could never hate,
Though sometimes they do seem

111

To suffer more
Than the common lot of man.

The Dioscuri disappear.

Theoclymenus   O, sons of Leda and Zeus,
For your sister's sake
I do renounce my quarrel
And if it is the will of heaven
That Helen should go,
Then so be it.
You have, I think,
The noblest and most virtuous   1860
Sister in the world.
Rejoice in her.
She was indeed rare among women.

war - waste of effort
life uncertain - fate?

NOTES

1 Theonoe (pronounced The-o-no-ee) means 'of godly mind'.
  Theoclymenus means 'of godly reputation'. As the story
shows, this is not at all an appropriate name for him, and so
may be seen as the first pointer to an important recurrent
theme: the difference between the appearance of things and
their reality.

2 'Stichomythia' – a dramatic convention whereby characters
speak to each other in alternate lines of verse – is used exten-
sively in *Helen*.

3 The story is told in Sophocles' play *Ajax*. It tells how a full as-
sembly of the Greek army voted to give Achilles' magnificent
armour to Ajax's great rival Odysseus. Incensed at the disgrace of this, Ajax planned to kill all the Greek leaders, but
Athene struck him with a fit of madness, and, unknowingly,
he slaughtered all their sheep and cattle instead. When the
madness left him, and he realised what he had done, the
added disgrace was too much for him and so he killed himself.

4 Helen's brothers are Castor and Pollux, the Dioscuri.

Accounts of them are contradictory. Here she says they are her father's sons, but later she calls them the sons of Zeus, and this is how they refer to themselves. Other sources insist that only Pollux was sired by Zeus.

5 Persephone (the maiden goddess of the spring) the daughter of Demeter (the goddess of the harvest) was stolen away by Hades, the lord of the underworld, and thereafter had to stay in his dark home for one third of each year. A *libation* was an offering of wine poured out in honour of the gods; hence, in this context, her tears.

6 The reference to Callisto is intended as a comparison with Helen's mother, Leda, who was also raped by Zeus. Callisto had a son, Arcas, and Hera was so furious that she changed her into a bear, which, according to Helen, was a kindlier fate than what happened to Leda. She might have mentioned that Zeus made amends to Callisto by placing her among the stars, where she became the Great Bear and her son the Little Bear.

7 The self-centred tedium of this opening is perfectly in keeping with Menelaus' character, which is typical of a certain type of army officer – rather boring and not very bright. The stories he refers to here tell of the beginnings of the House of Atreus, the most famous and ill-fated family in the whole of Greek mythology. It began with Tantalus, who hated the gods so much that he boiled his son Pelops in a cauldron and served him up to them to try and make them guilty of cannibalism, but the plan failed and Pelops was restored to life and Tantalus received his famous punishment. Later, Pelops' son Atreus did manage to trick his brother Thyestes into eating his own children! Atreus was Menelaus' father.

Pelops defeated Oenomaus in a chariot race and so was allowed to marry Oenomaus' daughter, the Princess Hippodamia.

8 The comedy begins. After all Menelaus' boasting we now see him being bullied and pushed about by one very old lady, and at one point he even seems to have started to cry.

9 Menelaus really is not very bright, nor is he very brave. When the Chorus appear it seems that he hides from them.

10 Menelaus has already apologised for the fact that he is in rags (l.490). Aristophanes, a writer of comedies, had made fun of Euripides for dressing his heroes in rags and tatters and this seems to be Euripides' answer. He repeatedly emphasises the fact, often playing it for laughs (l.627).

11 The recognition scene is a regular feature of romance, and Helen's ecstatic, lyric reaction, alternating with Menelaus' graver response, gives it an almost operatic quality.

12 This is sometimes used as a basis for suggesting that this is another of Euripides' anti-war plays, but it is too light-hearted and the Messenger is too comical a figure to carry such weight. Of course this version of the story would make the Trojan War a waste of effort, but that is part of the comedy, and is certainly part of the appearance-and-reality theme.

13 Calchas was a soothsayer in the Greek army. Helenus was his Trojan counterpart.

14 Just when everything seems to be going so well, Menelaus is thrown into confusion as the plot takes another comical turn on him.

15 The Chorus does well to wonder. Menelaus' speech is amazingly inept in every way.

16 The supposed death is another common feature of romance, cf. *Cymbeline* and *The Winter's Tale*.

17 It is not easy to see what the exact function of this chorus is, beginning, as it does, with a lyrical lament and ending with a fierce attack on the follies of war; but perhaps this very contrast, and the central passage on the uncertainties of life are simply meant to keep the audience guessing, because, unusually for Greek drama, the story was not well known and so the ending was in some doubt.

18 This scene has been full of ironies and ends on a splendid *double entendre*.

19 The relevance of this chorus has also been much debated. It tells the story of Demeter and Persephone (see also n.5), perhaps because, like Helen, Persephone was held against her will, and the Chorus here look forward to her freedom. Yet the chorus seem to confuse Demeter with Cybele, and the ending, which is textually corrupt anyway, does not seem to have a real connection with this part of the story at all.

20 This choric interlude is necessary to allow the action off-stage to take place, even though, in reality, it could not possibly happen in so short a space of time. However, the Chorus, in expressing their own longing to escape, send our minds out onto the seas.

21 Hyacinthus was a young Spartan who was accidentally killed by Apollo when they were throwing the discus together. A great midsummer festival was held in Sparta to commemorate the event.

22 The Messenger's speech relating events that had happened off-stage is a regular feature of Greek tragedy.

23 The *skene*, or stage-house, at the back of the acting area, had a device something like a crane whereby the gods could be lowered from its roof to 'earth'. Any final intervention, as here, by the gods to tie up the action of a play is, because of this, known as *deus ex machina* – when the god comes down on 'the machine'.

The Bacchae

The Legend
The Bacchae are the women followers of the god Dionysus. Dionysus is also known as Bacchus, but he is very different from the jolly, fat Roman god of the same name whom we see in the paintings of Rubens. In appearance, the Greek Dionysus was lithe, slim and sensuous, and although, like his Roman namesake, he was the god of wine, he was also very much more than that. He represented that special kind of vitality which we sometimes refer to as the Life Force. It is a force which, in itself, is neither good nor bad. It simply exists, and has, as the play shows, a potential for great beauty and contentment, but, on the other hand, has an equal potential for great cruelty and brutality, just as life has.

Dionysus was the last of the Greek gods to take his place among the other Olympians. He was the son of Zeus and Semele, the mortal daughter of Cadmus, King of Thebes, and what Euripides is depicting here, when Dionysus arrives in Thebes, is the arrival of the Dionysiac religion in Greece. That religion was an historical fact, and so, in terms of the experience at least, the play is semi-historical rather than totally legendary.

In the simplest possible terms, the Dionysiac religion involved, on the part of its followers, total and ecstatic self-surrender to the power of the god; this was something quite unacceptable to Pentheus, the puritan ruler of Thebes. He firmly denied the divinity of Dionysus, and the play relates the terrible fate he suffered as a consequence.

The Play
It is possible that Euripides never saw a performance of this, his last and greatest play, as its earliest known production was at Athens in 405 BC, the year after his death. For the last two years of his life he had been living in the mountainous region of Macedonia, in what was virtually a self-imposed exile.

Interpretations of the play have often differed widely. Some have seen it as honouring Dionysus, and suggest that after a lifetime of criticising the gods, the seventy-year-old Euripides was writing a death-bed 'recantation'; but the brutality of Dionysus' revenge is so horrific that, at the end of the play, our sympathy is surely on the side of his victims. Another view is that it is a total denial of the god, yet the lyrical beauty of the choruses seems to spring from a deep and personal religious experience. Both these views are really too extreme to be anything but wrong. Euripides has not taken sides. He has produced a work of art, not written a piece of propaganda. Propaganda has no lasting power, but this play has survived because of the power of its psychological understanding. It shows us the terrible consequences of a sudden outburst of emotion and how mass hysteria can shatter well-ordered lives that have been lived strictly according to reason. At the same time, it shows us the dangers of denying and suppressing such emotion. As Professor E. R. Dodds has written in his edition of the play: 'To resist Dionysus is to repress the elemental in one's own nature; the punishment is the sudden collapse of the inward dykes when the elemental breaks through perforce and civilisation vanishes.'

The Bacchae

CHARACTERS

Dionysus	
Chorus	of Oriental women, followers of Dionysus
Teiresias	an old blind prophet
Cadmus	founder of Thebes
Pentheus	grandson of Cadmus, now King of Thebes
Guard	
Herdsman	
Messenger	
Agave	daughter of Cadmus, mother of Pentheus

Outside the royal palace of Thebes. Darkness. A figure silhouetted against slowly growing light.

Dionysus   I ... am Dionysus, son of the king of gods,
Myself a god, wearing the borrowed body of
    man.
And this is Thebes, where Semele, my mother,
    died,
Burned at my birth by lightning.
There by the palace is her grave; and still
Over that ruined home where the divine storm
    struck,
The living fire of Zeus smoulders eternally,
A reminder of Hera's hate.[1]
It pleases me that Cadmus
Should have made this place a shrine
To the memory of her, his daughter;
And I myself have screened it round
With the clustering leaves of the vine.

I have come a long way. From Lydia and
    Phrygia,

118

The lands of the golden rivers,
Across the sun-baked steppes of Persia,
Through the cities of Bactria,
Smiling Arabia, and all the Anatolian coast,
Where the salt seas beat on turreted strongholds
Of Greek and Turk. I have set them all dancing;
They have learned to worship me   21
And know me for what I am:
A god.

      And now,
            I have come to Greece,
And first here, to my birthplace, Thebes.
Where already their women are shouting my
    name
In ecstasy. Their fine white bodies
I have clothed in fawnskins, and in their hands
Have put my thyrsus for a spear.[2]
For my mother's sisters...
Who of all women most owed me loyalty,
They would not have it that I *was* a son
Of god. 'Clever of Cadmus,' they said,
'Semele is got by her fellow with child,
And he fathers off her wantonness on Zeus.
But,' they sneered, 'the god would not tolerate
Such lies, and killed her.' For which sisterly
    malice
They are being rewarded. I have driven them
    mad,
And up onto the mountains, where they are wan-
    dering now,
Bereft of their wits, and there   39
I have thrust the badge of my service upon them:
All the women of Thebes I have driven from the
    city,
And there they sit with the daughters of
    Cadmus,
Far from their homes, and out of their minds,
Beneath the green pines, under the wide sky.
I shall teach this city a lesson

119

Its people may fear to learn;
They shall drink my service to its salt dregs,
And hear me speak for my mother Semele,
Then they will know the power that is Dionysus;
A god, son of a god, manifested among men.
Cadmus is getting old. He has relinquished his
    throne,
And has appointed as regent his grandson,
    Pentheus.
I am no god to Pentheus.
He pours out no libations before me;
Makes no mention of me in his prayers.
Therefore will I show him, and every Theban
With him, that I am indeed a god.
But once I have set things in order here,
And have established my rites, I will move on
And show myself in another country.
But should this city take arms against me   60
And try to drive the Bacchae from the hills,
Then I shall come with forces of my own
And lead them into battle.
But this I could not do in my own divine image,
So hide behind the likeness of a man.

Drums begin to be heard and get louder.

Come now, my followers out of the East,
You who marched with me out of Lydia
And the shadow of holy Tmolus,
Take up the Phrygian drums
That Rhea gave you, beat them now
As Cybele taught you, as *I* taught you
In the East;[3] beat them so this city of Thebes
May know that I am here.
Beat them while I return to the Bacchae
Waiting now on Mount Cithaeron,
And join their whirling dances.

Light dims. Dionysus goes out. Chorus enters.

Chorus   Over the holy Tmolus hill[4]
From Asia we came running

THE BACCHAE

With the lord god of laughter;   80
Our labour is joy,
Our weariness sweet,
For the song that we sing is to Bacchus.
          The song that we sing is to Bacchus.

Who's that in the street,
Who's hiding indoors?
Begone!
Let all other lips be still while we sing,
For the song that we sing is to Bacchus.
For the song that we sing is to Bacchus.
          The song that we sing
          The song that we sing
          The song that we sing is to Bacchus.

Happy is the man
Whom the gods have blessed
With a secret knowledge
Of their mysteries;
Who leads a holy life,
Sanctified by the ritual
Of the mountain dances;   100
Who observes the mystic rites
Of the mighty mother Cybele;
Who crowns his head with ivy;
And raises his thyrsus
High in the air
In worship of Dionysus.

Bacchae!
Bacchae!
Away, you Bacchae,
Bring back Bromius,
Our own true god,
The son of a god.[5]
Away, you Bacchae,
Bring back Dionysus,
Home from the Phrygian hills
To the spacious cities of Greece.
Away, you Bacchae,

121

THE BACCHAE

Bring back Dionysus,
Our own true god,
The son of a god.   120

When the pains of childbirth gripped Semele,
Zeus the Thunderer came.
His lightning pierced her side.
Bromius was born before his time.
Semele died.
But Zeus, the son of Cronus,
Found him another womb.
He hid him in his thigh,
Fastening him in with golden pins,
Safe from Hera's eye.
And when the Fates had formed him,
Zeus himself bore the bull-horned god;
He crowned his head with snakes:
Which is why the Maenads
Hunt down snakes,
And wind them about their hair.

Oh, join our dancing,
City of Thebes,
Thebes that cradled Semele,
Crown your head with ivy,   140
Bring branches of oak,
Sprays of fir,
And the scarlet berries of bryony.
Trim the fringe of your fawnskins
With tufts of white-fleeced wool.
Take hold of your thyrsus
But reverence it well,
The power of violence is there.
The whole world will soon be dancing,
When Bromius leads his revellers
Up to the mountains,
Where the women are waiting,
The Theban women
That he drove in frenzy
Out of their homes

122

Away from their looms.

In their secret cave
In the heart of Crete,
Where Zeus was born,   160
The great Corybantes
Stretched tight the hide-bound circle of the
    kettledrum
Kettledrum
                    Kettledrum
                                Kettledrum
That beat out the rhythm to the frenzy of their
    rites,
While the breathing sweetness of Phrygian
    flutes
Intoned the melody.

To the divine mother Rhea
They gave this drum
To complete the songs of the Bacchae,
But the crazy satyrs
Stole its tune
For the dance that they dance
When the third year comes,
The dance that delights Dionysus.

See the swift-footed Bacchae
Come running from the mountain tops of
    Phrygia,
The hills of Lydia,
Thirsting for the blood of the slaughtered
    goat,
The taste of its flesh in their teeth:
See the Dancer, wrapped in his sacred fawn-
    skin,
Surrender his senses to the spirit of the god, 180
And fling himself down in the sweet green
    grass;
The streams are flowing with milk and honey,
The springs are bubbling wine.
The fragrant scent of Syrian myrrh

123

Is wafted from the blazing pinewood torch
That the Dancer whirls in the air,
And the flames go streaming out as he runs,
Rousing the wandering bands of the Bacchae.
His silken hair is rippling in the wind
As he sets them dancing,
Dancing and running like that same wild
    wind,
And over their cries he shouts like the
    thunder:
'Evoe.[6]
Evoe.
Evoe.
Away, you Bacchae,
The glory and grace of golden Tmolus,
Hymn Dionysus to the rhythm of the drums,
With joy,
With laughter,   200
Praise Dionysus, the god of laughter.
Sing out the songs of Phrygia,
While the sacred and pure-toned flute
Adds its own merry tune
To the stamping of your feet,
As you rush on up to the mountains.'

The Dancer's voice goes echoing
                    Through the hills,
And every daughter of the Bacchae then leaps
    for joy,
Like a foal with its mother at pasture.

Enter Teiresias.

Teiresias[7]   Cadmus! Is anyone there?
Go and find Cadmus, someone,
Cadmus who built this city of Thebes.
Tell him Teiresias is here and wants him.
He will know what for. Old as we are,
We'll wear the sacred fawnskin,
And a crown of ivy too,
Just as we agreed.

124

Enter Cadmus.

Cadmus My dear old friend,
I knew it was you as soon as I heard you,
For a wise man has a wise voice. Well, here I am,
Dressed up for the part in the god's own
    costume.   220
We must do what we can to glorify his name,
    Teiresias.
He has shown himself a god, but he is the son
Of my own daughter too, remember.
Well, where do we go for the dancing then?
Come on, old oracle, read me the signs.
Oh, we'll dance and toss our old grey heads.
I could dance the whole night through
And not feel tired, yes, and the day as well,
Beating the ground with my thyrsus.
What a joy it is to be able to forget your age.

Teiresias You feel the same as I do then.
I too feel young again, young enough to dance.

Cadmus Shall I call for a chariot to take us up to the
    mountains?

Teiresias No, the god will think better of us for it
If we go on foot.

Cadmus   I'll be your guide then.
The old leading the old.

Teiresias   The god himself will
    guide us,
There will be no effort on our part.

Cadmus   Teiresias,
Are we the only men in Thebes
Dancing for Bacchus today?

Teiresias We are the only ones with any sense.   240
The others are all blinder than myself.

Cadmus Then what are we waiting for?
Take my hand. We mere mortals
Must not despise the gods of heaven.

Teiresias Our reasoning is little enough in their eyes.
The old, time-honoured customs
That our fathers have bequeathed to us
Cannot be overthrown by any subtle argument,

125

No matter what new logic
This clever age of ours invents.
People might think I had no sense of shame,
Going out dancing like this at my time of life,
With a crown of ivy on my head.
But no. The god did not say
That only the young should dance for him, or
    only the old.
He must needs be worshipped by all alike,
And all together...

Cadmus   Teiresias,
Since second sight's the only sight you have,
Let me interpret the signs of daylight for you.
My regent, Pentheus, Echion's son,   260
Is running here towards the palace,
And in a fine old fury too, by the look of him.

Enter Pentheus, attended by his guards.

Pentheus I was out of town when they brought the news to
    me –
Some strange disturbance in the city.
Our women, they say, have left their homes,
And gone cavorting about in the woods, on the
    mountain tops,
Religious ecstasy *they* call it.
Dancing in honour of some new-fangled god,
Some Dionysus – whoever he may be!
They seem to need a couple of skins of wine for
    it, too,
And when they've drunk their fill
They slink off one by one into the long grass
To find some man to lie with.
And *this* in the 'holy' name of Dionysus!
Dionysus! Aphrodite is more their level![8]
I've caught some of them already, though,
And had them locked up in the jail.
Those that are still at large I'll hunt   278
Down from the hills like the animals they are;
Ino, Autonoe, and my mother Agave with them.
Let them dance in prison with shackles on their legs.

126

And I'm told there's a stranger come to Thebes,
Some bogus magician from Lydia,
Some scented, golden-haired fellow
With a pink complexion and seduction in his
    eyes,
Who spends his days and nights with women
And young girls – teaching them the mysteries,
    as he calls it.
Let me once lay my hands on him here,
I'll stop him thumping his thyrsus and tossing
    his golden locks,
I'll have his head from his shoulders.
This, if you please, is the man
Who says that Dionysus is a god,
And was sewn up in Zeus's thigh,
When everyone knows that Dionysus was
    burned
In the same blast of lightning that killed his
    mother,
When she had the cheek to swear
That she had been bedded by Zeus.
Is hanging too good for such blasphemy,
Whoever this stranger is?   299

*(catching sight of Cadmus and Teiresias for the first
time)*

What ... on ... earth ... are ... you ... doing?
My own grandfather, with Teiresias the sooth-
    sayer,
Dressed up in fancy skins and playing with a
    magic wand.
Sir, this is beyond a joke.
Have you no more sense at your age?
Grandfather, take off that ivy,
And throw away that silly stick.

(turning on Teiresias)

This is all your fault, Teiresias!
A new god is a new source of income to you, isn't
    it?

127

More burnt-offerings, and more of your bird-
    watching!
By heaven! Only your grey hairs
Stand between you and the jail,
Along with the Bacchic women, for encouraging
These filthy rites. Mix wine
And women in a festival
And that festival, I say, is rotten.

Teiresias Give a man an honest case to argue
And he has no need of eloquence. You are glib,
But there is no sense in what you say;
And when a powerful man covers his folly
With a smooth tongue,
He is a danger, and a burden, to the state.   320

I have not words to tell you how great the glory
Of this new god will be throughout all Greece,
This god you mock.
                                There are two powers,
    young man,
Blessed to all mankind: first Demeter,
Or Earth, who brought us grain,
And then this son of Semele, whose gift of wine
Brings on that sleep that is the only medicine
For grief, and though a god,
He is himself poured out in our libations,
Himself an intercession and our prayer.
He is a prophet, too, this god;
And may so take possession of men's minds
That in their trance of Bacchic ecstasy
His worshippers foretell the future.
He also has a hand in Ares' work of war;
For Dionysus is there when you see an army
    under arms
Routed, and scattered by panic,
Before a single spear is raised.
                                One day
You will even see him at Delphi,   340
Bounding among the rocks, brandishing his
    thyrsus,

128

And whirling his pinewood torch in the air,
Great and renowned throughout Hellas.

Oh, listen to me, Pentheus,
Power is not all that matters in this life,
And if you are so foolish as to think it is
Then doubt your own sick thinking.
Welcome this god. Crown your head with ivy,
Dance, and pour out libations to his name.
Think how you like it when the crowd
Gathers at your gate, and goes shouting
The name of Pentheus through the streets.
Like kings, gods demand to be honoured.
So whether you laugh at us or not,
Cadmus and I are going to the dance,
A grey pair perhaps, but dance we must.
Nothing *you* may say could persuade me
To flout the gods in heaven, for you are mad,
Mad beyond curing.

Cadmus   My boy, Teiresias is right.
Your place is here with us,   360
And with our customs; do not
Go chasing your own wild thoughts.
Even if what you say is true
And Dionysus is no god,
It is not for you to say so.
It would be a great thing for our house
If Semele really was the mother of a god,
But if you cannot believe that,
At least lie for your honour's sake.[9]
You remember what happened to your cousin
    Acteon,
Who claimed he was a better hunter than
    Artemis?[10]
His own dogs avenged that boasting,
When they ripped him limb from limb
Out there on the mountain side.
Don't let that happen to you;
Here, let me crown you with ivy,
Then come with us, and glorify this god.

129

Pentheus Take your hands away! Go to your dancing,
But don't wipe your madness off on me.
By god, Teiresias here will pay for teaching you
To make yourself ridiculous.   381

Claps his hands and summons guard.

You,
Go to the throne where he sits and reads the
    auguries,
Take a crow-bar to it and turn it upside down.
Smash everything you see, and scatter
His garlands to the winds.
That will settle him.
                            You,
Search the city and the land outside,
And find this effeminate stranger
Who's defiling our women with his madness;
Find him, bind him, and bring him here to me.
He shall die by stoning. We'll see how he likes it
When Thebes does stage a dance in his honour!

He goes out.

Teiresias You fool! You reckless fool!
You don't know what you're saying!
You don't know what you're doing!
You were out of your mind before,
But now you are completely mad!
                            Cadmus,
We must go and pray for this misguided man,
And for our city. Take up your staff,
And give me your hand, lest we stumble.   400
We must go and do our duty
To the son of Zeus. But Cadmus,
I fear that Pentheus, whose name is sorrow,
Will indeed bring sorrow to all your house.[11]
This is not prophecy, but common sense.
That foolish man is no wiser than his words.

THE BACCHAE

They go out.

Chorus Holiness, queen in heaven,[12]
Holiness, gliding on golden wing
Over the face of the earth,
Did you hear that unholy mortal,
That miserable king of Thebes?
Did you hear him insulting Bromius,
The son of Semele, the god of joy,
Bromius who sits at the head of the table,
Whenever the gods in heaven are merry
And garlanded for their feasts?
He taught us the sacred dances.
He quickened our feet with the music of flutes.
He brought us cups of wine and we drank
Them down and we slept, and in our sleep we
    forgot   420
Our cares, and in our dreams we were gods.
A hasty word can lead to a bitter end.
The wise man guards his tongue,
Escapes the storm, and keeps his house
    secure.
Far away though the gods may be
They watch us just the same.
Cleverness is not wisdom.
This life is short, and meddling
In the gods' affairs may make it shorter still.
Only a madman would reach so high
That he dropped what he had in his hand.

Oh, to set sail for Cyprus, Aphrodite's island,
Domain of the Queen of Love, where spells
    are made
To charm men's hearts, and sweeten their
    brief lives;
Or to that land where the fertile river
Licks its seven tongues over the arid sand
Till it gets the taste of corn.
Take me, Bromius, to where I can see
The holy slopes of Olympus, the grass is

131

greener there,
Sweep down to Pieria.   440
Take me to the home of the muses.
Teach me to worship, teach me to laugh,
Where the Bacchae are free to practise their
    rites
With the Graces and sweet Desire.
Dionysus, the son of Zeus, is a god who loves
    the feast,
And he loves that mother of youth,
The divine benefactress, Peace.
He brought wine for the rich and the poor
To slake the thirst of their grief,
But he will not stand for the pompous man,
Too proud to accept his gift, who turns down
This lifetime's chance of health and happi-
    ness.
A delight in the simple things is the creed
In which we, his disciples, believe.

*Enter Guard, with Dionysus bound. Pentheus comes out
to them.*

Guard Our hunt is over, Pentheus, and here we bring
    back
The prey you sent us out to catch.
But this 'wild beast' was tame, my lord.
He did not hide, or try to run away;
He gave himself up quite willingly.
He was not afraid either. He just smiled   460
And told us to bind him and lead him away.
He even stood still to make it easier for us.
I felt ashamed, and told him,
'Stranger, it's not that I want to arrest you,
I'm only acting under the king's orders.'
And there's another thing, my lord.
Those women you had chained up in jail,
They have escaped, and gone back to the hills,
Dancing and calling on Bromius their god.
The chains just fell from their feet,

And the bolts slid back on the doors;
No one had touched them. This stranger
Has worked many miracles in Thebes.
But that is not my concern.

Pentheus Untie his hands. Now that I have him in my net,
He is not so nimble that he shall get away from
me.

*Pentheus looks his prisoner up and down as the guards
untie him.*

You're not unhandsome, are you, stranger?
No doubt you appeal to women –
But, of course, that's why you are here.
Not the born athlete, I take it,   480
With that long silken hair tumbling down your
cheeks?
And such clear, white skin – you must have
taken
Great care of it, avoiding the sunlight,
And walking in the shadows, but then the
shadows
Are always more conducive to lust, aren't they,
stranger?
Now, who are you, and where are you from?

Dionysus You have heard tell of the flowery slopes of
Tmolus?

Pentheus The hill that curves round Sardis? Yes, I know
it.

Dionysus I come from there. My country is Lydia.

Pentheus Then how do you come to be preaching this new
religion in Greece?

Dionysus Dionysus, the son of Zeus, initiated me in it.

Pentheus Oh, you have a Zeus that begets new gods now
and then, have you?

Dionysus No. He is the same Zeus that married Semele
here in Thebes.

Pentheus Did he come to you in a dream, or in broad daylight?

Dionysus Face to face, and he gave me emblems as proof.

133

Pentheus	What are they like, these emblems?
Dionysus	None but initiates must know.
Pentheus	Have they any special value to initiates, then?
Dionysus	It is not permitted you to know, though it is worth knowing. 499
Pentheus	You are trying to whet my curiosity, aren't you?
Dionysus	No. The mysteries of the god are not for the impious.
Pentheus	You said you saw him face to face. What form did he take?
Dionysus	Whatever form he wished. I could not order it.
Pentheus	What sort of answer is that? Again you evade the question.
Dionysus	Even the wisest answer seems foolish to a fool.
Pentheus	Is this the first place you've brought your new religion to?
Dionysus	Foreigners everywhere are dancing to Dionysus.
Pentheus	Foreigners haven't the sense of Greeks.
Dionysus	In this at least they have more. Customs differ, that is all.
Pentheus	Tell me: do you worship by day or by night?
Dionysus	Mostly at night. Darkness is more fitting for devotion.
Pentheus	More fitting for lechery too.
Dionysus	Men sin by daylight if they wish.
Pentheus	You shall pay for this insolence.
Dionysus	You shall pay too, for your blasphemy.
Pentheus	Oh, you are a brave priest, but a bit too ready with your tongue.
Dionysus	What punishment have you in mind? What is my fate to be?
Pentheus	First, I will cut off all your delicate curls.
Dionysus	My hair is sacred and dedicated to the god.
Pentheus	Then your wand. Give it here. 520
Dionysus	You must take it yourself. Only Dionysus can give it to you.
Pentheus	And you'll be locked up in the jail.
Dionysus	The god himself will free me whenever I choose.
Pentheus	When you call on him in your dancing? Not here –

Dionysus He is *here* now, watching what I endure from you.

Pentheus Where is he? I can't see him.

Dionysus Here, where I am. It is your impiety that blinds you.

Pentheus (*to Guard*)

Take him away. He is making a mockery of me and the whole of Thebes.

Dionysus I warn you. Do not bind me.

Pentheus I am the one who gives orders here. Bind him!

Dionysus You do not know the limits of your power.

You do not know what you are doing, nor who you are.

Pentheus I am Pentheus, son of Agave and Echion.

Dionysus Pentheus – 'The Child of Grief' –

An apt name with which to meet *your* fate.

Pentheus Take him away. Lock him in the stables.

If he wants to dance in the dark,

Let him dance there. That ought to be dark enough.

The drums begin rising to a crescendo.

As for these women you've brought here

As your accomplices, I'll sell them abroad as slaves,   540

Or put them to work at my looms

In the palace. I'll silence the intolerable

Beating of their drums.

He goes out.

Dionysus I will go.

What is not to be, I cannot possibly suffer.

But Dionysus, whom you deny,

Will take revenge for this impiety.

Your chains fall on a stranger,

But you manacle a god.

Dionysus is led away.

135

Chorus   O blessed maiden,[13]
Queen of the waters,
Dirce, child of Achelous,[14]
Once your springs
Welled up their waters,
Eager to wash
The son of Zeus,
When his father snatched him
Out of the roaring flames,
Hid him safe in his thigh,
Shouting, 'Come, Dithyrambys, come,
Into your father's womb.
Bacchus I'll call you,   560
When I reveal you
Thebes will rejoice at your name.'

But blessed Dirce,
When I came
To dance within your land,
You shut your ears to my song,
You tore the flowers from my hair.
Oh, why do you shun me,
Why do you scorn me,
Why do you send me away?
I swear by the vine's full glory,
I swear by my lord of roaring,
You will remember this day.

Child of the dragon's teeth,
Earth-born son of Echion,
Pentheus shows his breeding.[15]
This is no man but a monster,
Born to challenge the gods.
Our leader is locked
In a gloomy dungeon.   580
How can the servants
Of Bacchus escape?
Dionysus! The whip of oppression
Is tearing the flesh from our backs.
Dionysus, can you see us?
Come down with your golden thyrsus,

Come down from the heights of Olympus,
Put an end to this murderous man.

Are you leading your revellers,
Thyrsus in hand,
Over the slopes of Nysa?
Are you leading them safe
From the tiger's claw
Through the ragged peaks of Corycia?
Or perhaps in the glades of Olympus,
Where Orpheus gathered the wild beasts
And the trees, with the sound of his lyre?

Pieria, Bacchus delights in you.
Over the foaming Axius river
He comes with his Dervish Dancers,   600
He comes to set you dancing.
Over the streams of Lydia,
Father of all the waters,
A blessing to all of men,
Streams that flow through emerald fields,
Where famous stallions graze,
Bacchus is dancing over these fields.
Bacchus is coming.

Voice of Dionysus   Hear me, Bacchae! Hear my cry!
          Chorus   What was that?
                       Where did it come from?
                       It was the voice of Dionysus, his ritual call.
Voice of Dionysus   Again I call, the son of Semele and Zeus.
          Chorus   Hail, Master! Hail, Bromius!
                       Join our company, Lord Dionysus!
Voice of Dionysus   Lord of the earthquake, shake the floor of
                       the world!
          Chorus   (*individual voices*)
                       See, the tyrant's palace is about to fall.
                       Soon the walls will crack,
                       The roof will crash to the ground.
                       Dionysus storms in the hall!   620
                       Bow down before him.
                       Humbly we bow.
                       See where the flames leap high

On the holy tomb of Semele.
The flames of Zeus.
Look where the lintels dance on the doorposts.
The palace is loud with the voice of god!
Bow down!

Voice of Dionysus Come down, lightning ablaze, blasting
The palace of Pentheus! Strike and destroy!

The lightning flashes. Darkness. The women of the Chorus scream and fling themselves to the ground. Sound of the roof crashing down. As the peal of thunder which brought darkness dies away, light returns. Dionysus is standing in the middle of the prostrate Chorus.

Dionysus Were you so frightened, my poor friends,
That you threw yourselves down on the ground?
You must have seen then
How the palace of Pentheus tumbled
At the touch of the god. But come,
Rise up. Do not be afraid.

Chorus How glad we are to see you again,
Our leader in the holy dance.
We were lost and helpless without you.

Dionysus Were you afraid when they took me away,   640
And cast me into prison?

Chorus Where could we turn for help if you were taken?
But how did you escape?

Dionysus I was my own saviour.
There was no difficulty.

Chorus But were you not chained to the walls?

Dionysus I even made a fool of him there.
He thought he was tying me up.
But he was wrong.
He never even touched me!
He was going to lock me up in a stall,
But when he got there
He found a bull and tied the rope

138

Round the bull's knees, not mine.[16]
He was biting his lips, dripping with sweat,
And panting with rage all the time,
While I sat by and watched.
Then Bacchus came,
And shook the building in his hands,
Making the flames on his mother's altar   660
Blaze up in the air, and the king,
Thinking that the palace was on fire,
Went rushing this way and that,
Shouting to his servants to bring more water
Till the palace was in an uproar,
And all for nothing!
Then he thought I'd got away,
And stopped what he was doing,
Snatched up his sword and dashed off into the
          palace.
Then Dionysus made a phantom appear
– Or so it seemed to me –
For I only tell you what I thought I saw.
And Pentheus flung himself at it,
Stabbing away at the bright air,
Thinking all the time that he was killing me.
But Bacchus had not finished with him yet.
He smashed down the palace
Leaving it in a heap of rubble;
My fetters must be a bitter sight to Pentheus
          now.
He has dropped his sword;   680
Worn out and exhausted.
He, a mortal, tried to do battle with a god;
But I came out of the palace untouched,
And here I am. Pentheus does not worry me.
He will be here in a moment, I think.
What will he say now?
Never mind, for all his fury, I'll face him.
It's a wise man who keeps his temper.

Enter Pentheus.

Pentheus   It's an outrage! That man I had in chains,

139

	He's escaped, he's . . . You!
	How did you get out? Answer me.
Dionysus	Stop where you are. Wait for your temper to cool.
Pentheus	How did you get out? How did you get past my guards?
Dionysus	Didn't I tell you, or weren't you listening,
	That someone would set me free?
Pentheus	Who is this mysterious 'someone'?
	Stop saying things I don't understand.
Dionysus	He who made the clustering vine,
	And gave it to man.
Pentheus	A fine answer that is. 700
Dionysus	You insult his greatest gift.
Pentheus	Whose?
Dionysus	Dionysus'.
Pentheus	Did he set you free? Where is he?
Dionysus	He is still close at hand.
Pentheus	Bar the gates!
	Shut every exit from the city!
Dionysus	Do you hope to imprison a god?
	Could he not pass over, or even through, your walls?
Pentheus	You are so wise, so wise,
	In everything except where you should be.
Dionysus	Where I most should be, there I am wisest of all.
	But someone is on his way here
	From Mount Cithaeron. First
	Listen to the tale he has to tell.
	Don't worry. I shall not run away.

Enter a Herdsman.

Herdsman	My lord, my lord Pentheus,
	I have come from Cithaeron,
	From below the ridge which the snows
	Fall on, and . . .
Pentheus	Get to the point, man.
	What is your news?
Herdsman	I have seen the Bacchae, my lord,
	The women who ran barefoot from the city. 720
	I have seen their madness, and the awful,

140

Weird, and miraculous things that they do.
I have come to tell you and the whole city
About it, my lord, but ... I fear your royal
    temper;
Have I leave to speak freely?

Pentheus Speak. You have nothing to fear from me,
Whatever your story is. My anger
Is not for the innocent. But the worse your
    account
The worse it will be for the man
Who first bewitched our women.

Herdsman I was working my cattle up to the high
    pasture,[17]
Just as the diamond dew flashed
In the first rays of the morning sun,
When I saw three groups of women. Autonoe led
    one,
Your mother, Agave, another, and Ino the third.

Stretched out in the long grass they slept,
Pillowed on oak leaves, bedded in pine needles,
Limbs loose as they had flopped to their rest,
Modestly though, not as you told us,
Not drunk on wine, worn out from dancing,   740
Not making love in the secrecy of the woods.

But Agave, at the sound of my cattle,
Sprang up in their midst with a long,
Loud cry that woke them, and they, as one,
Leaped to their feet, rubbing the sleep
From their eyes – a marvel of order
And a strange sight. Old women, young ones,
Girls still unmarried, their hair tumbling
Over pale shoulders, gathering their fawnskins
About them, girdling the dappled fur
With snakes that licked their faces
As they tied them round their waists.
Some in their arms held young gazelles
And wolf cubs, giving them to suck
Of their own white milk,
Their newborn babes abandoned in their
    cradles,

141

So that their breasts were full.
One struck her thyrsus against the hard rock,
And a spring of crystal water spurted out,
Another plunged her wand into the earth,   760
And a fountain of wine leaped into the bright air.
Those who thirsted for milk had only to scrape
The ground with their fingers and it was there.
Sweet streams of honey dripped from the
    thyrsus.
If you had seen the works of this god for yourself
You would offer up prayers, not curses.

But up there on the hillside we held a meeting,
Shepherds and herdsmen, arguing over the
    strange,
Uncanny things we had seen, and one chap,
A town lad with the gift of the gab, took over as
    usual,
And said to us, 'Comrades of this holy mountain,
Why don't we do the king a bit of a favour,
Hunt down his mother, get her away
From these orgies, and take her back to Thebes?
It ought to be worth our while.'
It seemed a good plan then,
So we laid in ambush to wait our chance;
And when the time came they began to dance;
In the wake of their dancing all things stirred.
The cattle prancing, the dumb rocks sang,   780
Till the mountain itself came under the spell.
And Agave chanced to pass near me.
I broke from my hiding, grabbed at her heel,
But she saw me and screamed,
'Watch out, my hounds, we are hunted by men,
Let your wand be a spear in your hands,
Arm yourselves then,
And follow!'
And we fled for our lives,
Or they'd have torn us limb from limb.

As it was, our cattle stood in their way,
As they swept on down the hill.

A bellowing heifer with swollen udders
Was seized by one frail girl;
It lay helpless in her hands.
Others were tearing our cows apart.
Ribs and hooves were flung into the air,
And strips of bloody flesh hung dripping from
    the trees.   800
Proud bulls of the herd, with fury in their horns,
Were thrown to the ground by a thousand
    hands,
And the flesh was stripped from their bones.

Then down, swift as swallows,
They ran, skimming the ground, down
To the fields of golden corn
That grow by the river Asopus.
Down like an army they swept
On the villages under the Cithaeron ridge,
Hysiae and Erythrae, plundering as they went,
Snatching the children out of their homes.
Up on their shoulders they tossed their loot,
Burdens of bronze and iron,
And not one single thing was dropped;
And on their heads they carried fire,
And not one single hair was burned.

The villagers rose up in arms at this pillage,
And went for the Bacchae with spears,
But a strange thing happened then, my lord,
Their sharpened weapons drew no blood,
Yet the thyrsi in those women's hands
Cut deep into their flesh,   820
And women put men to flight.

Then gently they made their way back to the
    hills,
To the springs that their god had made;
And washed the scarlet blood from their hands,
While the snakes licked the stains from their
    cheeks.
Whoever this god may be

143

His powers are great, my lord;
Welcome him to your land.

Pentheus It is here, and spreading like a fire,
This obscene dancing; now violence;
A disgrace to the whole of Greece.
It has got to be stopped.
Go to the Electran Gate and summon my guard.
Call out every man fit to carry a shield,
My spearmen, bowmen, cavalry, everyone!
It is past bearing that women
Should inflict such shame upon us.

Herdsman goes out.

Dionysus You never listen to what I tell you,
Do you, Pentheus? But, I will give you
One more warning, in spite of the way you treat
    me;   840
Do not take arms against a god.
Calm yourself. Bromius will never
Forgive you if you drive his women
Away from the echoing hills.

Pentheus Don't you preach at me.
Remember you have escaped from my prison.
You had better be careful, unless
You want me to punish you again.

Dionysus If I were in your place,
I would sooner make sacrifice to the god,
Than foolishly try to do battle with him.

Pentheus Yes, I'll make him a sacrifice,
Those women of his will be a lavish sacrifice,
When I slaughter them in the woods on
    Cithaeron.

Dionysus You heard. You will all be routed.
Think of the disgrace – a whole army
Defeated by women; your bronze shields
Dashed from your hands.

Pentheus   Where am I
To turn with this man? In jail or out
He's never quiet.   860

Dionysus   Pentheus, there is still time

	To settle this peacefully.
Pentheus	How? By becoming the slave of my own slaves?
Dionysus	I will bring the women back here Without bloodshed or force of arms.
Pentheus	This is some trap.
Dionysus	How can it be a trap, When I am ready to save you By my own devices?
Pentheus	You are all in league. You have made a pact with them to establish Your rites here for ever.
Dionysus	I have made a pact – I don't deny it – a pact with the god.
Pentheus	Bring me my armour! I've heard enough from you.

Pentheus strides away, but when he is almost off-stage Dionysus shouts at him, and from now on begins to dominate him. [18]

Dionysus	Wait! Would you like to see them as they sit Huddled together on the mountain side?
Pentheus	I would give all the gold in my treasuries.
Dionysus	Oh? And why this sudden and unnatural longing?
Pentheus	I would be sorry to see them maddened with wine.
Dionysus	Yet you are eager to see what you know would upset you?
Pentheus	Yes, if I could hide under the trees, without a sound. 880
Dionysus	They will track you down however carefully you hide.
Pentheus	Then I will go openly. Yes, you are right.
Dionysus	If I lead you, are you ready to go?
Pentheus	At once.
Dionysus	First you must disguise yourself as a woman.
Pentheus	*What? Me* dress up as a woman? Never!

145

THE BACCHAE

Dionysus   If they knew you were a man they would kill you.
Pentheus   Yes ... yes ... of course, you're right again.
How clever you've been all along.
Dionysus   Dionysus taught me.
Pentheus   What will be the best way to go about it?
Dionysus   Come inside and I will help you to dress.
Pentheus   Dress? A woman's dress? No, it's humiliating.
Dionysus   Don't you want to spy on the Bacchae any
longer?
Pentheus   Yes, but ... what must I wear?
Dionysus   A wig of long hair to cover your own.
Pentheus   And then?
Dionysus   Robes to your feet and a hood over
your head.
Pentheus   Go on.
Dionysus   A thyrsus in your hand, and a fawnskin.
Pentheus   I cannot do it. I could not   899
Bring myself to wear such a womanish costume.
Dionysus   You will only cause bloodshed
If you fight the Bacchae.
Pentheus   That's true.
I must go and spy on them first.
Dionysus   That is wiser than chasing one evil
With another.
Pentheus   But how can we pass
Through the city without being seen?
Dionysus   I will guide you through the side streets.
Pentheus   Anything as long as those women
Don't laugh at me. I must
Make up my mind.
Dionysus   I will do
whatever you decide.
Pentheus   I will go inside and
think.
Perhaps I will lead my army against the
Bacchae,
Or perhaps I will follow your advice.

Pentheus goes out.

Dionysus   The man is walking into the net.

146

He shall see the Bacchae and shall pay the price
With death.
                        Now, Dionysus, it is for you
To take up the action. You are not far away.
Punish this man. Steal away his reason,
And plant fantastic madness in its stead.
In his right mind he would not consent   920
To such a scheme, but drive his senses from him
And for all those fierce threats of his
I will parade him like a woman through the
        streets,
And make this king the laughing stock of
        Thebes.
Now I will go to dress him for the ritual,
In the clothes he must wear
When he goes down to hell,
Slain by his mother's hand.
In that moment he will know
What Dionysus is –
A god terrible to man,
And yet, most gentle.

Dionysus goes out.

Chorus Shall I ever again dance all night long,[19]
With my white feet bare,
And my head thrown back in the cool night
        air,
Like a fawn at play
In the green field's joy,
That slipped the chase, and the eager hands,
Leaped the net,
And got far away?   940
But the hunter calls again to his hounds,
The straining pack is on to its prey,
And down by the water's edge she runs,
The speed of the wind in each aching limb,
Till she's safe at last in the silent trees,
Where the leaves hang thick,
And the shades are dim.

What then is wisdom?

What god-given gift could please man more
Than to raise his hands in victory
Over the head of a conquered foe?
Honour is precious and always will be so.

Though slow be its advance,
Yet surely moves the power of gods,
Correcting mortals mad with pride
Who disregard their words.
Subtly they lie in wait,
Throughout the length of time
To trap the godless man.
It is not wise   960
To override their laws
In action or in thought.
It is a maxim cheaply bought
That whatsoever heaven may be
There the glory lies,
And what the centuries decree
Is lawful now,
And will forever be.

What then is wisdom?
What god-given gift could please man more
Than to raise his hands in victory
Over the head of a conquered foe?
Honour is precious and always will be so.

Happy is the man whose fragile boat
Rides out the storm at sea,
And safely makes the port.
Happy is he who triumphs over trial.
One man in many ways, in wealth and
    strength,
Outdoes his friend, and countless hearts
Have each their seed of hope,   980
Some will bear fruit
And others die away;
But the truly happy man
Is he who best enjoys
Each passing day.

Enter Dionysus.

Dionysus Pentheus, so eager to see forbidden sights,
Crazed, impious, reckless Pentheus! Come out,
And let us see you in your woman's dress.
A madwoman, a Bacchante, a spy, a seeming
Daughter of Cadmus, tracking the daughters
Of Cadmus.

*Enter Pentheus: he now appears as though hypnotized,
and completely in the power of the god.*

Pentheus Two suns ... two cities ... each
With seven gates ... everything seems double
 now.
Are you a bull walking before me,
With horns on your head? Yes,
I think you are a bull; perhaps
You were an animal all the time.

Dionysus The god is with us. He was angry before,
But now he is friendly. Now   1000
You see as you should see.

Pentheus What do I look like?
Does not Ino, or my mother Agave, stand like
 this?

Dionysus Just like that. You might be
A Bacchante yourself. But be careful,
Your hair is falling loose.

Pentheus I must have shaken it down
When I was practising the dance
Just now in the palace.

Dionysus I will put it right for you.

Pentheus Yes, for I am in your hands now.

Dionysus And your girdle needs tying; the hem
Is uneven there by your ankle.

Pentheus It is all right on this side though.

Dionysus You will count me as your friend,
When you find how chaste the Bacchae really
 are.

Pentheus Does a Bacchante hold her thyrsus
In her right hand, or like this?

149

THE BACCHAE

Dionysus	In the right hand. You raise it as you raise
	Your foot, keeping time with the dance.
	What a change has come over you.
Pentheus	I could lift Cithaeron on my shoulders,
	Its valleys and all the Bacchantes with it.
	Could I do that?
Dionysus	If you wished.
	It was your thinking that was weak before,
	Now you are strong.
Pentheus	Shall I take a crowbar with me,
	Or shall I tear the hills apart with my hands,
	Toppling the peaks with my shoulder?
Dionysus	What? And destroy the homes of the mountain
	spirits,
	The haunts of Pan, where he pipes on the cliff?
Pentheus	You are right. We must not use force
	On women. I will hide in the pine trees near
	them.
Dionysus	I will find you a hiding place
	That befits a spy.
Pentheus	I can almost see them now
	Entwined in their lust,
	Like mating birds in a thicket.
Dionysus	And for that you must set watch over them.
	You might even catch them –
	If they do not catch you first.
Pentheus	Lead me in triumph through the streets of
	Thebes.
	I, and only I, have the courage for this deed.
Dionysus	You, and you alone, bear their burden.
	And the reward will be worthy of you.
	Follow me. I will guard and guide you
	Till we are there – but another
	Will bring you home.
Pentheus	My mother[20]
Dionysus	An example to men...
Pentheus	It is for that I go.
Dionysus	You shall ride home...
Pentheus	Sweet triumph!
Dionysus	In your mother's arms.

1040

150

Pentheus	You will spoil me!
Dionysus	She will spoil you.
Pentheus	My courage deserves no less.

Pentheus goes out.

Dionysus How strange and terrible you are!
And so terrible the death you go to
That its fame will tower from here to heaven.
Stretch out your hands, Agave,   1060
And you, daughters of Cadmus.
I bring the young prince to his final trial,
Where the victors will be god, and I.
Now time must tell the tale.

Dionysus goes out.

Chorus Dogs of madness[21]
Fly to the mountain top,
Where the daughters of Cadmus
Are holding their rites.
Drive them to frenzy of rage
At the madman
Who puts on a woman's clothing
To go and spy on their dance.
His mother will see him
Behind some boulder,
Or peering down
From the top of a tree;
And she'll cry to the Bacchae:
'Which of the sons
Of Cadmus is this
Who comes to the mountain,   1080
Runs to the mountain,
To spy on the dancing daughters?
What womb could have born him?
No woman's blood
Could produce such a man!
This is the cub of a lioness,
Or rather a Libyan gorgon!'

151

THE BACCHAE

Let Justice walk the earth,
Let Justice come with a sword
And plunge it deep in the throat
Of this shameless, lawless, godless,
Son of the earthborn Echion.

Look at him, Bacchus,
Blind to reason
And twisted with rage
At your great powers
And your mother's mystery.
Off on a madcap scheme he goes
To try out his strength   1100
On the invincible.
Man must be humble
And remember his place,
If he really wants
To live in peace.
I would not begrudge
The wise their wisdom,
But happiness comes with purity.
Pure by day
And by night too,
Honour the gods
And they will honour you.

Let Justice walk the earth,
Let Justice come with a sword
And plunge it deep in the throat
Of that shameless, lawless, godless,
Son of the earthborn Echion.

Come, Dionysus,
As a roaring bull,
Or a hundred-headed cobra.   1120
Come like a lion
Snarling fire,
Down on the hunter of the Bacchae.
Smile at him, trick him,
Then trip him in a noose
And hurl him screaming

152

THE BACCHAE

Under the stampeding feet of the Bacchae.

Enter Messenger.

Messenger	Weep, lament for the house,
	The house that is fallen!
Chorus	What is it?
	Do you bring news?
	News from the mountain?
Messenger	Pentheus, the son of Echion, is dead.
Chorus	Hail, Bromius! Hail Bacchus!
	How mighty a god
	You show yourself!
Messenger	Do you shout for joy at his fate?
Chorus	For joy, yes; we are free now.
	In my own tongue I can shout,
	'The oppressor is dead.'
	Your chains have no terror now. 1140
Messenger	Do you take us for cowards?
	Do you think Thebes has no men left?
Chorus	Thebes has no king to threaten us.
	Dionysus is our king.
Messenger	Rejoice then in your freedom,
	And may the gods forgive you,
	For a noble heart would feel some pity.
Chorus	How did he die?
	Did the sinner die in his sin?
	Tell us about his death,
	Tell, tell, tell.
Messenger	When the last farm of Thebes was behind us,
	And we'd crossed the river Asopus,
	We began to climb the foothills of Cithaeron.
	Pentheus, me, his attendant, and the stranger
	Who was to lead us to what we were to see.
	First we lay down in a small clearing.
	We kept quite still, never a whisper,
	So that we could see, without being seen.
	We were in a deep valley, with cliffs 1160
	On either side, and running streams
	Shaded with dark pine.

153

And there before us were the Maenads,
Some entwining their thyrsi with fresh ivy,
Others, happy as foals set free from the harness,
Were singing their Bacchic songs.
But Pentheus could not see them and said,
'Stranger, from where I am
I can't make out these so-called Maenads,
But on that bank up there,
Or if I climbed a tree,
Then I could clearly see their goings-on.'
And then I saw the stranger work a miracle.
Reaching up to the topmost, towering
Branch of a mighty tree he drew it down,
Down and down to the dark earth,
Bending like it like a bow, like a circle,
Like when you take a peg and line
And trace a wheel rim out upon the ground.
He took that pine tree in his own hands   1180
And bent it to the ground.
It was a miracle.
Then he set Pentheus in its branches,
And let it slip slowly though his hands,
Gently so as not to throw him off,
Until it rose sheer into the sky,
The king perched on the top of it,
So the Bacchae could see him
Better than he could see them.
The tree had hardly finished quivering
When the stranger disappeared, and a voice,
That must have been Dionysus,
Shouted down from heaven,
'Women, I bring you the man who mocked you,
The man who mocked me and my holy rites.
Now you can take your revenge.'
And as he spoke a sheet of flame
Fell down to earth.
The air went still.
The whispering of the leaves was hushed,   1200
And not one single sound was heard.
At first, the women, unsure of his voice,

154

Sprang up and looked around,
But he called again,
And they knew it was their god.
Swift as doves they darted forward,
Agave, the mother of Pentheus,
Her sisters and all the Bacchae,
Up the valley, along by the stream
And over the rock they went leaping,
Their spirits possessed by the god.
And when they saw where Pentheus was,
They climbed to the top of the cliff,
And pelted him with rocks.
Branches of pine and their thyrsi
They flung like javelins;
The king sat there – trapped and helpless;
But the tree was too high,
And try as they would
Their shots fell short.   1220
So they tore down branches of oak,
And, using them as levers,
Tried to heave it out by the roots,
But it was no use.
So then Agave cried,
'Gather round, you Maenads,
This climbing-beast must be caught
Before he betrays our secrets.'
And seizing the tree in their hands
They wrenched it from the earth,
Till down from its branches,
Screaming loud as he fell,
Plunging and crashing to the ground,
Came Pentheus. Agave fell on him,
And, like a priestess,
Began the ritual of death.
He snatched the band from his hair,
So she would know him,
And spare him.
He touched her cheek, crying,   1240
'Mother, it's me your son,
I know I've done wrong, but have mercy,

You surely can't kill your son.'
Agave was foaming at the mouth.
Her eyes were rolling wildly.
She was possessed.
She would not listen to him.
She grabbed hold of him by the wrist,
Stuck her foot in his chest,
And ripped his arm off from the shoulder.[22]

It was not her strength, but the god's.

Ino and Autonoe set on him,
Tearing his flesh with their nails,
And the whole throng of the Bacchae
Was screaming in triumph.
Pentheus screamed too
With what breath was left in his lungs.
One ran off with an arm;
Another with his foot,
The shoe still on it.   1260
His ribs they stripped and clawed clean,
Their hands thick with blood,
As one to another they tossed his flesh
Like children playing with a ball.
His body lies scattered among the rocks,
And in the depths of the woods.
It will not be easy to find.
His head – his head – his mother has,
Fixed on the point of her thyrsus,
Carrying it over the mountainside,
As though it were the head of a lion.
She has left her dancing sisters
And is on her way here to the palace,
Rejoicing in her prey,
Calling on Bacchus her fellow-hunter
And partner in that chase
Whose prize can only be tears.
I cannot stay to see such a sight.
A contrite humble heart
Is the wisest thing a man can have,   1280
If he will only use it.

Chorus	Glory to Dionysus!
	Bacchus we praise you,
	And render thanks
	For the fall of Pentheus,
	The spawn of the serpent,
	Who dared to dress
	In the clothes of a woman,
	And take in his hand
	The sacred Thyrsus
	That guided him down to hell;
	A bull he had
	To lead him to his fate.
	Daughters of Cadmus,
	Slaves of Cadmus,
	Great is the song of victory
	You have begun...
	But you will finish it in tears.
	What sport to embrace
	Your own child, your hands 1300
	Thick with his blood.
Agave	(*off-stage*)
	Bacchae!
Chorus	But listen! Listen!
	She is coming...
	Agave, the mother of Pentheus...
	Her wild eyes staring...
	Prepare to receive the progress
	Of a triumphant god!
Agave	(*off-stage*)
	Bacchae! Followers of Dionysus!
Chorus	What do you want with us?

Enter Agave running. She carries Pentheus' head fixed on the point of her thyrsus. Her dress is torn, and she is covered with blood.

Agave	I bring to this palace
	A new-cut garland fresh from the mountain.
	Happy our hunting!
Chorus	We see. We see. Welcome.
	Hail, fellow-worshipper!

157

Agave	Without a snare I caught it.
	See the whelp of a mountain-lion!
Chorus	Where?
Agave	Cithaeron.
Chorus	Cithaeron?
Agave	We killed it there.
Chorus	Who first struck home?
Agave	Mine is the fame!
	On the mountains the Bacchae shout my name –
	Agave – the blessed!
Chorus	Who else?
Agave	It was Cadmus...
Chorus	Cadmus?
Agave	Whose daughters laid hands on the prey,
	But after me! Oh after me!
	Happy our hunting. Come share in the feast.
Chorus	Oh, pity! How should we share it?
Agave	Look, the bull is so young,
	The soft hair on its jaws is scarcely grown
	Under the flowing mane.
Chorus	The hair indeed might be that of a beast.
Agave	The god is cunning,
	And cunningly set his hunters
	Onto the prey!
Chorus	Our lord is a mighty hunter.
Agave	Do you praise me now?
Chorus	Can we praise you?
Agave	Soon the men of Thebes...
Chorus	And Pentheus, your son?...
Agave	He too will praise his mother
	When he sees what she has done.
	Making the lion's whelp her prey!
Chorus	A strange prey.
Agave	And strangely captured!
Chorus	Are you glad?
Agave	I exult! My heart is full
	For the great and wonderful
	Victory of the chase!
Chorus	Poor wretch! Show then to all the city
	The trophy you have won.

1320

1340

158

Agave   (*coming down to the audience*)
You who dwell in the turreted citadel
Of Thebes, come closer that you may see the
    prey
We, the daughters of Cadmus, hunted down and
    killed.
We. had no nets, or spears,
Only our own white hands, our delicate fingers –
What have men to boast of who go to armourers
To forge them useless weapons of bronze?
With our bare hands we caught the beast
And tore its limbs to tatters.
Cadmus? Where is my father? And where is
    Pentheus,   1360
My son? Call him. Fetch him. He must display
Over the palace gate my lion's head.

Agave goes out.
Enter Cadmus, with attendants carrying Pentheus' body
in a sheet.

Cadmus   Come, bring the unbearable burden that once
Was Pentheus home. Lay it down there
Before the palace. Oh, I am tired –
Tired of endlessly searching through the glens
Of Cithaeron, where his body lay in pieces –
In pieces, strewn and scattered among
The depths of the forest, no two parts together.
Teiresias and I had just returned from the
    dancing
When a man told us what my daughters had
    done,
So I hurried back to the mountain, and now
    fetch home
The body of my son whom the Bacchae killed.
There among the oak-glades I saw Ino and
    Autonoe,
Still wandering wildly to and fro, possessed
By the spirit. But Agave, they said,
Had turned homeward, and is here before me.

Agave   (*entering with the head of Pentheus in her arms*)

159

	Father, now you have a right to be proud!	
	For you have the bravest daughter in the world!	
	Yes, all your daughters, but me above all,	1380
	For I left the loom idle for nobler things,	
	To hunt wild beasts with my bare hands!	
	Look! Look at the trophy I hold!	
	It is mine; I won it alone; I brought it	
	For you to nail up over the gate of the palace.	
	Take it, Father, take it, and invite your friends	
	To a feast to celebrate my triumph in the chase!	
	For you are blest, Father, blest	
	By this deed I have done!	
Cadmus	I dare not look upon the thing that you have done,	
	The slaughter your wretched hands have made.	
	A fine victim to sacrifice to the gods!	
	A fine feast you ask me, and the city, to attend!	
	Oh, how I pity you, my daughter, and pity myself.	
	The god has destroyed us.	
	We sinned, it is true, but could he not show	
	A little mercy to his own house?	
	Can he be a just god when he is so, so cruel?	
Agave	How old age has soured you, Father,	
	And withered the smile from your eyes!	1400
	Oh, I hope my son takes after his mother	
	And becomes as great a hunter. He must ride out	
	With all the noble youth of Thebes	
	Slaying the wild beasts instead of wasting his strength	
	In battle with the gods. You must speak to him, Father.	
	Call him here, someone, so that he can see	
	What his mother has done. I want to hear him praise me!	
Cadmus	Dear god, when once you know what you have done...	1440
Agave	What has gone wrong? What troubles you?	
Cadmus	Look there, look hard at the sky.	
Agave	What is there to see?[23]	

Cadmus	Do you see ... no change in it?
Agave	It seems a little brighter than it was, less cloudy.
Cadmus	And is your mind still in that state of ecstasy?
Agave	I don't know what you mean. But I can Think clearer, somehow. I feel ... as though I've changed.
Cadmus	Can you hear what I am saying, then? Can you give an intelligent answer?
Agave	Father, I can't remember what we've just been saying.
Cadmus	Who was your husband? 1420
Agave	You gave me to Echion the earth-born.
Cadmus	Who was the son you bore him?
Agave	Pentheus.
Cadmus	What, then, is the head you hold in your arms?
Agave	We were hunting it ... they said it was a lion.
Cadmus	Look at it then – come, it is easy enough to look.
Agave	What is it, Father, what is in my arms?
Cadmus	Look at it, and find out what it is.
Agave	No. It's something terrible. Oh, god!
Cadmus	Does it look like a lion now?

Cadmus forces her to look at it. She gives a long-drawn-out sobbing cry.

Cadmus	Now there are two to bear the pain.
Agave	Who killed him? How does this come to be in my hands?
Cadmus	Oh, Truth, this is no place for you.
Agave	For god's sake, tell me. My heart is tight with terror.
Cadmus	You and your sisters killed him.
Agave	Where was he killed? At home or where?
Cadmus	Where once Acteon was torn to pieces by his dogs.
Agave	Cithaeron? Why did he go to Cithaeron?
Cadmus	To insult Dionysus, and to mock your dancing.
Agave	But we, why were we on the mountain?
Cadmus	You were possessed. The whole city was pos- sessed.
Agave	I understand. Dionysus has destroyed us.

161

Cadmus	He was insulted. You denied his divinity.
Agave	Where is his body, Father?
Cadmus	After much searching I have brought it home.
Agave	Is it all decently laid together?
	I was mad, but why should Pentheus suffer?

She goes to the body.

Cadmus Like you, he would not reverence the god,
And so the god has brought destruction on us all,
You, your sister, and your son.
He has destroyed our house, and with it me
Who had no sons, only this boy, the child
Of your unhappy womb; and now he is dead,
Horribly and shamefully killed.

The whole house looked up to him.
Our dry stock took hope from him.
Child of my child, you were a terror to the city,
For no one who saw you would have dared
To face your wrath by insulting my old age.
I, Cadmus the Great, who sowed the seed
   whence sprang   1460
The world's noblest harvest – the men of
   Thebes.
Oh, my dear child – for even in death
No man is dearer to me than you –
Never again will you touch my cheek,
Put your arms around me and call me 'Grand-
   father',
And ask, 'Has anyone wronged you or insulted
   you,
Has anyone annoyed you, or made you angry?
Tell me, so that I can punish him for not respect-
   ing you.'
But now I am ruined, and you destroyed,
Your mother in torment, and her sisters
   wretched.
If there be any among you
That hold the heavens in scorn,
Look now on this man's death
And so believe.[24]

162

THE BACCHAE

A growing rumble of drums. A light pours on them from above.

Chorus See where the intense light catches the eastern
sky!
It is Dionysus, the Bull of God,
Revealed a god among men!

Voice of Dionysus Oh, all you people of Thebes,
Fall now and worship me!   1479
I am Dionysus, son of Zeus and Semele,
Denied by you,
Revealed among you now.
Pentheus opposed me, and has met
The death that he deserved.
You trifled with my power,
And now reviled and punished
You must bear the cost of that transgres-
sion.
Had you but had the wit to understand
You would know now the bliss and not the
bitterness
Of serving such a god as me.[25]

Cadmus Dionysus, we implore you; we confess our sins.

Voice of Dionysus It is too late. At the proper time
You would not know me.

Cadmus We have learned, but you are too exacting.

Voice of Dionysus I am a god, and I was spurned.

Cadmus But it is not right that gods, like men,
Should be vindictive.

Agave It is all over, Father. We are outcasts now.

Dionysus Why, then, delay what cannot be evaded?

The light fades.

Cadmus Oh, my child, it is an evil day that dawns for us,
For you, for your unhappy sisters and for me.
A stranger among strangers I must end my days.
There will be no end to my sorrow.   1503
Not even Acheron, the river of death,
Will bring me peace.

Agave puts her arms round his neck.

163

THE BACCHAE

Agave	Oh, Father, where shall I go When they drive me from my home?
Cadmus	I do not know, child, Your father is no use to you now.
Agave	Then goodbye, my own dear land.
Cadmus	Go quickly, my daughter, To where your sisters are waiting At the house of Aristaeus.
Agave	It is a shameful thing The Lord Dionysus has done.
Cadmus	It is a shameful thing he suffered. His name had no honour in Thebes.
Agave	Farewell, then, Father.
Cadmus	Farewell to you, my child, Though how should you fare well?

1520

Cadmus goes out.

Agave	Lead me, friends, to where my sisters wait To share my exile. I long to be where never again Cithaeron shall look down on me, Where never again shall dread Cithaeron Loom upon my sight, Where I shall find no thyrsus To call memory back. Others must dance for the Lord Dionysus now.

Agave goes out.

NOTES

1 Hera was the wife of Zeus.
2 A *thyrsus* was a staff topped with a pine cone and wreathed around with ivy. As Dionysus was a kind of male fertility god, this symbol which his followers carried no doubt had phallic connotations.

3 Rhea was called the 'mother of the gods'; her children included Zeus, Poseidon and Demeter. Cybele was a Phrygian Great Mother Goddess figure. Her priests, the Corybantes, worshipped her with shouts and cries, and drums and clashing cymbals.

4 The Chorus: Dionysiac worship is the basic theme of all the choruses, and each one may be seen as reflecting the mood of the god. The entrance chorus takes the form of a kind of cult hymn. As well as telling the story of Dionysus' birth, it is a song of joy, expressing the ecstatic but gentler aspects of their religion.

5 Dionysus is also known as Bacchus and as Bromius, and as Dithyrambys. The Bacchae are also called Maenads (see line 134), meaning 'mad women'.

6 Evoe: this cry is untranslatable, so has been retained simply as a sound.

7 Teiresias is the religious leader of Thebes – an old, blind prophet.

8 Aphrodite was the goddess of love. Pentheus constantly suspects that their rites involve orgies. He is a puritan with a strong prurient streak. It is this weakness that Dionysus plays on later, and which sends him to his death.

9 Cadmus and Teiresias are not genuine believers. Both act out of expediency. Cadmus thinks what a grand thing it would be to have a god in the family, and Teiresias, a professional priest, is aware of the advantage of being part of a promising new religion.

10 Acteon was one of Pentheus' cousins. As well as the very ill-advised boasting mentioned here, it is also said that while he was out hunting once he chanced to see Artemis, the virgin huntress-goddess, when she was bathing naked. In her anger, she turned him into a stag and he was torn to pieces by his own hounds – a warning of what is to happen to Pentheus.

11 Pentheus' name means 'child of grief'.

12 This chorus is a commentary on the previous scene and on the folly of Cadmus and Teiresias – 'Cleverness is not wisdom'. But their mood is still one of gentleness.

13 The Chorus are disturbed by Pentheus' behaviour, and a sense of urgency is felt as they call on Dionysus for help.

NOTES

> There is a psalm-like quality here, reminiscent of one of the songs of tribulation.

14 Dirce was the wife of an earlier ruler of Thebes. She was murdered and her body thrown into a spring which was later called by her name.

15 The story of the founding of Thebes tells how Cadmus first fought and killed a dragon and was then told by Athene to sow the earth with the dragon's teeth. He did so, and armed men sprang out of the ground where the teeth fell.

16 The bull is one of the animals always associated with Dionysus, reflecting his vitality and power.

17 The herdsman's speech clearly shows the dual nature of the Dionysiac religion. First there is the peace and tranquillity of an almost paradisal scene, but it is followed by the most bloodthirsty violence.

18 This scene, in which Dionysus begins to dominate Pentheus by playing on his emotional instability, shows Euripides stepping out of the world of legend and into a new area of genuine psychological awareness.

19 The Chorus begin to show their power.

20 Euripides has a fondness for ironies of this kind.

21 A savage song of vengeance, preparing us for the tale the Messenger is about to tell.

22 This kind of violence could only be given us by report; it could not possibly be staged.

23 The power of this 'recognition scene' rests in its very simplicity.

24 At this point in the play some fifty lines have been lost. From quotations and fragments surviving elsewhere it seems likely that they included a lament from Agave, but no attempt has been made here to reconstruct the speech or to suggest what it might have been.

25 No play can more clearly demonstrate that blend of pity and terror which Aristotle said were essential ingredients of the end of a tragedy.